I0756391

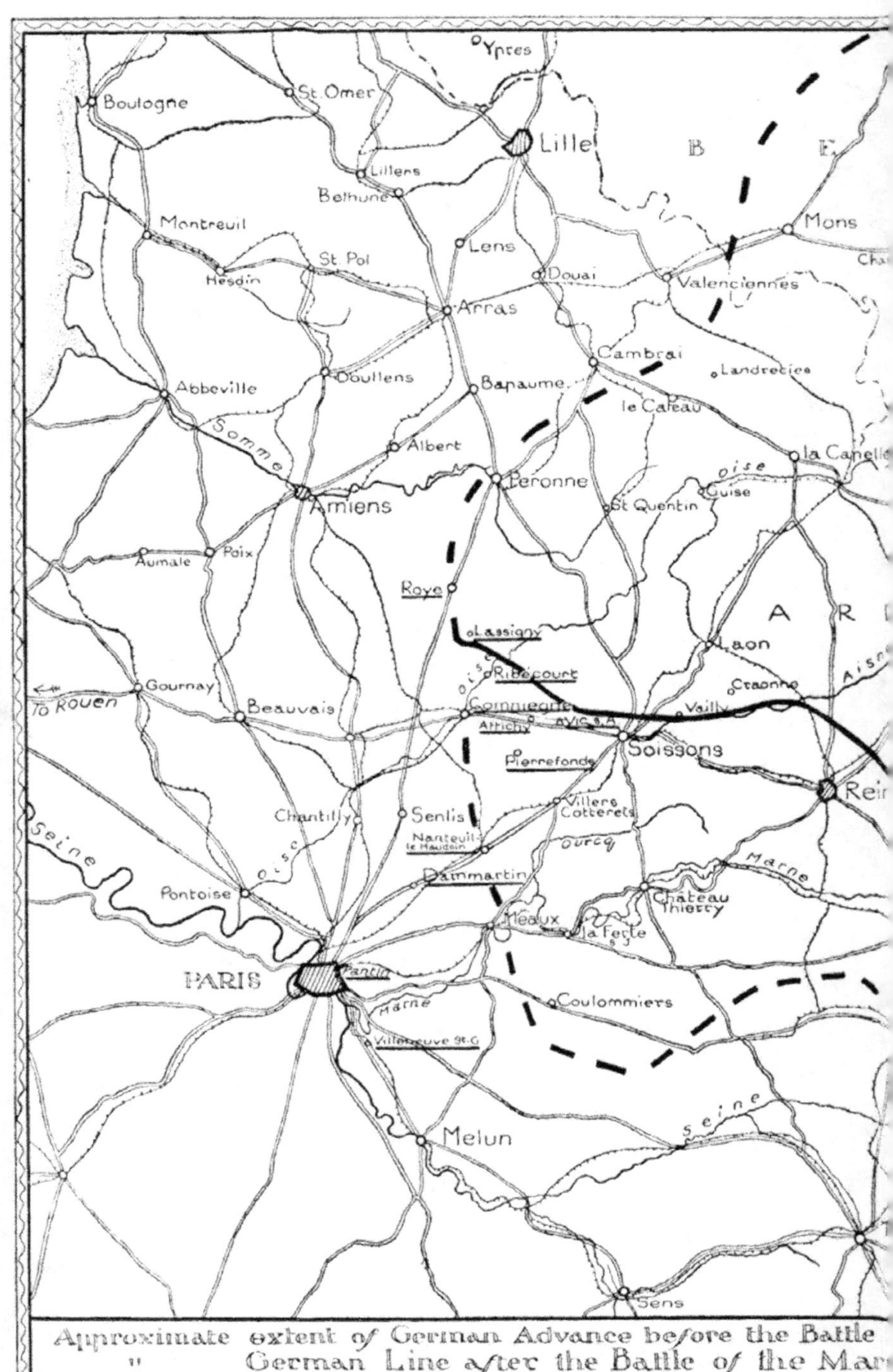
Ypres
Boulogne
St. Omer
Lille
B
E
Lillers
Bethune
Montreuil
Lens
Mons
St. Pol
Hesdin
Douai
Valenciennes
Arras
Cambrai
Landrecies
Doullens
Abbeville
Bapaume
le Cateau
Albert
Somme
la Capelle
Peronne
Oise
Guise
Amiens
St Quentin
Aumale
Poix
Roye
A
R
Lassigny
Laon
Ribécourt
Gournay
Craonne
To Rouen
Beauvais
Oise
Compiegne
Vailly
Attichy
Soissons
Pierrefonds
Villers Cotterets
Chantilly
Senlis
Seine
Nanteuil-le Haudoin
Ourcq
Marne
Oise
Dammartin
Pontoise
Chateau Thierry
Meaux
la Ferte
PARIS
Pantin
Coulommiers
Marne
Villeneuve St-G
Seine
Melun
Sens
Approximate extent of German Advance before the Battle
" German Line after the Battle of the Mar

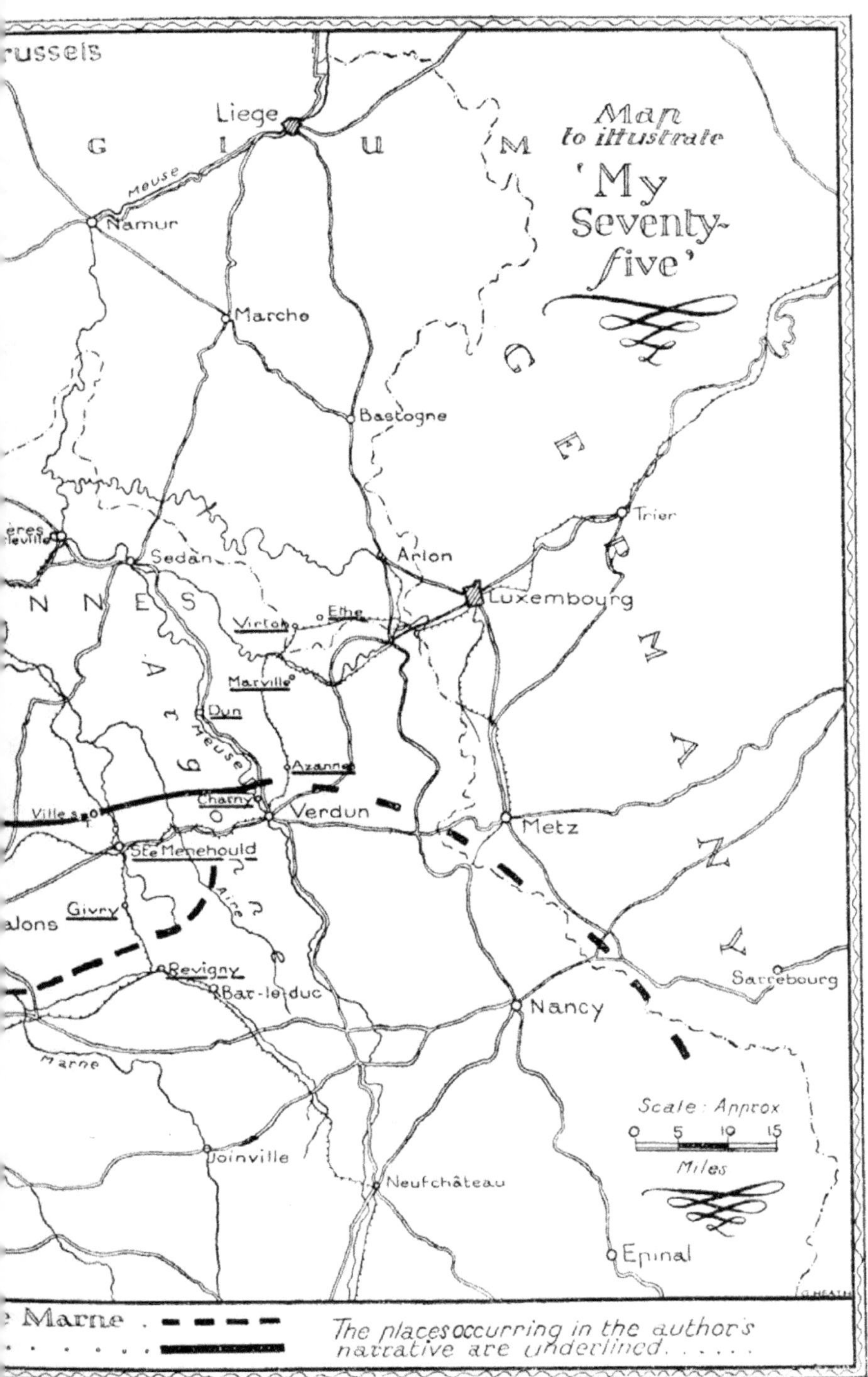

Map to illustrate 'My Seventy-five'
russels
Liege
G I U M
Meuse
Namur
Marche
Bastogne
G E R M A N Y
Trier
Arlon
Luxembourg
Sedan
N N E S
Virton
Ethe
Marville
Dun
Meuse
Azannes
Charny
Villes
Verdun
Metz
Ste Menehould
Aire
Givry
alons
Revigny
Bar-le-duc
Nancy
Sarrebourg
Marne
Joinville
Neufchâteau
Epinal
Scale: Approx
0 5 10 15
Miles
Marne
The places occurring in the author's narrative are underlined. . . . .

SOLDIERS' TALES

MY SEVENTY-FIVE

SOLDIERS' TALES.

Uniform with this volume.

A SUBALTERN'S WAR.
(Somme 1916–Ypres 1917.)
By Charles Edmonds.

With Introductions by the Hon.
Sir John Fortescue

MEMOIRS OF SERGEANT BOURGOGNE (1812–13).

PASSAGES IN THE GREAT WAR WITH FRANCE (1799–1810).
By Sir Henry Bunbury.

JOURNAL OF THE WATERLOO CAMPAIGN.
By Cavalié Mercer.

RECOLLECTIONS OF RIFLEMAN HARRIS.

LIFE AND ADVENTURES OF MOTHER ROSS.
By Daniel Defoe.

NOTE-BOOKS OF CAPTAIN COIGNET.

ADVENTURES IN THE RIFLE BRIGADE.
By Captain Kincaid.

ADVENTURES IN THE REVOLUTION AND UNDER THE CONSULATE.
By Moreau de Jonnès.
Translated by C. E. Hammond.

In preparation.

THE ADVANCE FROM MONS, 1914.
By Walter Bloem, *Captain, 12th Brandenburg Grenadiers.*

Mobilisation.

(A 75 mm. gun, Versailles, August 1914.)

MY SEVENTY-FIVE

JOURNAL OF A FRENCH GUNNER
(August – September 1914)

by

PAUL LINTIER

With a Foreword
by
MARSHAL JOFFRE

The Naval & Military Press Ltd

Published by

The Naval & Military Press Ltd
Unit 5 Riverside, Brambleside
Bellbrook Industrial Estate
Uckfield, East Sussex
TN22 1QQ England

Tel: +44 (0)1825 749494

www.naval-military-press.com
www.nmarchive.com

In reprinting in facsimile from the original, any imperfections are inevitably reproduced and the quality may fall short of modern type and cartographic standards.

TO THE MEMORY

of

CAPTAIN BERNARD DE BRISOULT

who fell with his face to the enemy
and whose death wrung tears
from the scorched and powder-blackened eyes
of his men

Ce livre écrit par un jeune engagé volontaire qui mourut en Mars 1916, *sur le front de Lorraine, est d'un poignant intérêt.*

Il est le vivant et sincère témoignage des efforts, des fatigues, et des innombrables dangers que les soldats Français ont supportés, sans faiblir, au cours des premiers mois de la Grande Guerre, qui furent les plus sanglants et les plus durs de cet immense conflit.

Il met en lumière les magnifiques qualités de ces hommes qui avaient compris que de leur discipline, de leur volonté et de leur courage, dépendait l'existence de la Patrie. Et c'est aux vertus dont ils firent preuve que nous avons dû la Victoire.

Je suis heureux de leur renouveler ici le témoignage de ma reconnaissance et de ma paternelle affection.

Paris,
le 8 *mai* 1929.

TRANSLATOR'S PREFACE

PAUL LINTIER was killed instantaneously by a shell on March 15th, 1916, at Jeandelincourt on the Lorraine front, being then a sergeant of artillery and in his twenty-third year. Only four days earlier, in the intervals between bombarding and being bombarded, he had revised the proofs of *Ma Pièce*;[1] the book was published in the following month, and has ever since been accepted in France as the truest and most illuminating account, from the point of view of the ranks, of that first phase of the war which Englishmen recall by the names of Mons, the Marne and the Aisne.

The outbreak of hostilities found Lintier in barracks at Le Mans, a gunner with something less than a year's service. Born at Mayenne in 1893, and originally destined for a commercial career, he had chosen letters instead. In his student days at Lyon he had founded the *Lyon Etudiant*, a literary review in which his first essays appeared; and when, in the autumn of 1913, he enlisted in the 44th Artillery Regiment, he had already three short volumes to his credit, and was regarded by all who knew of him as a young writer of the most brilliant promise.

He had begun work, in the leisure hours of army routine, on two novels which were to have been his first serious contribution to literature. But the events of July 1914 interrupted these labours, and provided the

[1] *Ma Pièce: Avec une Batterie de 75: Souvenirs d'un Cannonier, 1914.*

young soldier-author at the same time with an alternative opportunity. Clearly foreseeing the drama which was about to be enacted and in which he was to play a part, he determined to be, within the limits of the vision afforded him, its historian. And from the actual day of mobilisation (August 1st) he kept a detailed journal of events, and continued it faithfully day by day until September 23rd, when he was admitted to hospital with a severe shrapnel wound in the right hand. The result was, and is, a series of unflinchingly exact and impressive scenes, by means of which we are enabled to accompany a French soldier and his comrades, to share their thoughts, see what they saw and feel what they felt, throughout the first eight critical weeks of the war.

Since the journal is historical as well as personal, it may be useful to review the movements of Lintier's battery in relation to the general campaign on the Western Front.[1] Entraining at Le Mans on August 8th, they reached Charny, five miles north of Verdun, on the evening of the next day, and thence marched northwards across the Belgian frontier in time to be present with the 4th Corps of the Third French Army at the Battle of Virton (August 22nd). The effect of this battle, as of the almost simultaneous Battles of Mons and Charleroi far to the north-west, was to demonstrate the strength of the invading forces in a manner as forcible as it was unexpected. During the advance of the British Expeditionary Force into Belgium, bets had been freely and light-heartedly made on the probability of occupying Berlin before Christmas. In the French Armies also "*A Berlin!*" was the cry, perhaps rather more grimly uttered; the theory of an irresistible attack had long predominated in the minds of our Allies, and hopes of a swift and crushing *revanche* ran high. Such miscalculations, no doubt, were normal enough; it must be in the

[1] A table of the chief events, August–December 1914, will be found on pp. xxiv–xxv.

nature of things for both sides to go to war in a spirit of optimism.

The great retreat which followed instead brought bitter disillusion; it was a retreat which began, so far as Lintier's part in it was concerned, with something very like a rout at Virton, and it continued thereafter so ominously and with such constant pressure from the enemy as to fill the minds of almost all men with the direst misgivings. The hardships and hazards of our own retreat from Mons are well known; it must be remembered that the tribulations of the French Armies were not only similar but on a far wider scale, and that all the time they were being forced to abandon their own countryside, their own burning towns and villages, many thousands of their own women and children to the mercies of an ancient foe. Comparison of 1914 with 1870 was unavoidable.

Lintier's battery, then, bearing its full share of rearguard actions—it was now that the famous *soixante-quinze* guns first proved their worth—retired some seventy miles in thirteen days, arriving on September 4th at Révigny-aux-Vaux in the Department of the Marne. The day before, a civilian had informed Lintier that the Germans were through Compiègne and thus within forty miles of Paris. General de Langle de Cary's Fourth Army now effected a partial relief of the hard-pressed Third Army, enabling the 4th Corps to be withdrawn; and the depleted battery, with one gun out of action, racked with doubts and fears, and worn out, both men and horses, with their tremendous exertions and with violent diarrhœa, entrained that night for an unknown destination.

At the end of a long, slow, depressing journey they found themselves, on the morning of the 6th, approaching Paris from the south-east. Passing through Villeneuve-Saint-Georges—the station was full of British troops—they finally detrained at Pantin, on the northern outskirts of the capital, and marched a short distance into billets at Rosny-sous-Bois. News came to hand meanwhile that the Germans had advanced beyond Creil, only twenty-five miles due north along the Boulogne and Calais railway; while from Rosny the fighting on the Grand Morin, eastwards, was clearly audible. The Battle of the Marne had begun.

Next day General Joffre's famous order calling on his armies to turn and attack the invader reached them; and on the same night they marched north-east along the main Soissons road. On the morning of the 8th they were in action near Sennevières, a few miles beyond Dammartin, being now in General Maunoury's newly assembled Sixth Army, operating on the immediate left of the British Expeditionary Force and having as its primary function the containing of the German right wing.

The following day, the 9th, was critical. Lintier and his comrades knew well that the fate of France hung in the balance, and what they saw of the battle was far from reassuring. They worked appalling execution on the enemy, but he still advanced in seemingly irresistible numbers; the infantry in front of them retired; the guns had to be switched completely round and fired to the rear; night fell on what they all felt must have been still another defeat. At any instant they expected orders to retire at full speed from their exposed position, leaving Paris itself and heaven knew how much more of France in the enemy's hands. It was a bad moment, and even Captain de Brisoult, of whom Lintier draws so fine a portrait, could not entirely hide his anxiety.

No better example could be found of the limited vision of individual soldiers or units in a great battle. The reverse, which to them seemed a disaster, was purely local. They were near the left and most forward flank of a sixty-mile battle-front along which, on that and the three previous days, Joffre had made good his historic counter-stroke. His armies and the small British Army had turned at last, taking advantage of von Kluck's change of direction, and Galliéni had sent up his last reserves from Paris in a fleet of taxi-cabs—Lintier had a glimpse of them—all with decisive effect. On the strangely quiet morning of September 10th an infantry battalion came along the road, advancing; and its commander gave the weary gunners the glorious and totally unexpected news that the Germans were in full retreat.

The battery advanced in its turn over a corpse-strewn plain that bore witness to the devastating accuracy of their fire, and through towns and villages littered with evidence of the brief German occupation and of the abruptness of the enemy's departure. How could they help believing, in common with thousands of worn but exultant Frenchmen and Englishmen, that the enemy was about to be driven out of France as quickly as he had come in? . . . They crossed the Aisne on September 13th at Vic, fourteen miles west of the left flank of the British Army at Venizel, and came into action at various points on the high ground beyond; where the line was to be stationary, almost without change, for four grisly years.

For the inconclusive Battle of the Aisne, as everyone knows, resulted in a deadlock and was the beginning of trench warfare. As soon as this became apparent, each of the two opposing armies tried to outflank the other northwards; and the outcome, within a few weeks, was a continuous line of trenches as far as the Channel coast. Lintier saw only the commencement of these manœuvres. His battery was withdrawn back across the Aisne on September 18th, and moved round, in conjunction with the Maroccan Division, through Pierrefonds and Compiègne to the left of the Allied line. On the 22nd they were fiercely engaged between Lassigny and Noyon. As the action developed the enemy's counter-battery work became more and more accurate, and Lintier was one of the first casualties. The journal comes to an end with his admission to hospital on the following day.

That Lintier should have managed to keep a full journal throughout the arduous campaign of which an outline has been given seems almost a miracle, when we consider that except for a few days spent with the waggon-lines (by no means a rest-cure) he was all the while an active "gun-number." But there is no doubt that he did so, and that these are, essentially, the day-to-day record of his thoughts and experiences. He kept a second journal [1] on his return to the Front in July 1915, which was found on his body, complete to within a few hours of his death. The fact, too, that at so early an age he was promoted sergeant and died in command of a gun, is proof of the thoroughness with which he performed his duties. The truth must be that he was born to write; he had to. "I have never left off writing my notes every day," he says in a letter to a friend. "It's an excellent form of discipline; the best I know. Apart from the fact that these notes will be terribly 'lived,' I find them of the utmost value in helping me to keep myself in hand. Nothing else could have so steadying an effect. . . ."

And it is this strict contemporaneousness that gives *Ma Pièce* its peculiar importance in the literature of the war. It has none of the inevitable vagueness of retrospection; it is the immediate reaction of a distinguished and acutely observant mind to the war—the soldier's war—as it really was. "*Ces notes puent la vérité*," they reek of truth, as a prominent critic (M. Willy) has declared; nor will any soldier deny the statement. Of the book's other merits the reader will naturally form his own judgment; but of this he may rest assured, that

[1] *Le Tube 1233 : Avec une Batterie de 75 : Souvenirs d'un Chef de Pièce (1915–1916).*

Lintier, whether he is describing a night-march, the sensation of being under fire, a field of battle, the gun in action, a heap of corpses, or any aspect of the soldier's life, is describing only what he himself saw and felt, and what is absolutely true.

For the rest, *Ma Pièce* was at once hailed as a work of outstanding excellence when it was first published in France. And a phrase from M. Pierre Mille's review of it in *Le Temps* may be quoted here, since it very concisely explains why the book is still read and re-read after the lapse of thirteen years. "This superb book," said M. Mille, "is the work of a great writer. If you want to see the frightful reality of the war, here it is for you. There is a quality in the writing, a natural, instinctive talent, a proud detachment of outlook, which gives you the war as it will appear to our grandchildren: legendary and immense."

A perfectly just appreciation, but one that M. Mille would doubtless have qualified had he been writing in the latter part of 1916 or in 1917, by which time the 1914 fighting had already become almost legendary. He would then have said "the frightful reality of the first phase of the war." For there was a difference: in those later years the war acquired new frightfulnesses and shed nearly every other attribute. In 1914, certainly, it was bad enough; particularly in the matter of casualties, which in the abortive French offensives at the very outset were terrific. But it still had movement and variety; the French infantry wore red trousers then, and carried colours into action; the uniforms of chasseurs, cuirassiers, zouaves were brilliant against green summer landscapes; traces of the ancient glamour clung persistently to the war of 1914, and it was still intensely dramatic. Indeed, to a man who has taken part in a great, open-warfare battle, such as those so graphically described by Lintier, all subsequent excitements are likely to prove tame; though he may prefer it so. What soldier of the later times has forgotten the longing for a "break-through" and "open warfare"? And in this sense those first ten weeks may well be regarded as typical of earlier wars rather than of the "Great War" itself, the slow, drab war of trenches, dense barbed wire, creeping barrages, featureless mud-landscapes, poison gas, intensive counter-battery bombardments, half-trained soldiers and "advances" of a few hundred yards in a month of incessant fighting.

But if the true and particular loathsomeness of the war hardly revealed itself until after the Battle of the Aisne, and reached its zenith, let us say, at Verdun and Passchendaele,[1] that is not to say that 1914 had not horrors in plenty. It was, on the whole, the most critical time of all, when the odds seemed heaviest against the Allies; and it was then, nevertheless, that by feats of courage, endurance and downright, grim fighting which were certainly never surpassed and perhaps never quite equalled afterwards, the ultimate victory was made possible. No wonder the men who performed this service, our own "Old Contemptibles" and the French by whose side they fell, became invested with a special heroism of their own.

Lintier was one of them, and like so many of them, he was killed. It is generally agreed that in him France lost a great writer; but the picture which he left of

[1] Without in the least ignoring First and Second Ypres, Neuve Chapelle, the Aubers Ridge, Loos, the Somme, etc., and their French parallels. But there was an upward curve to the points mentioned, partly because of the increasing numbers fatally involved, partly because of the reiterated futility, and partly because each later battle was shadowed by the accumulated gloom of its forerunners. "Oh, forget September the Third," as Mr Blunden expresses it in his masterpiece; and there was a feeling abroad during Third Ypres that a man could nowhere dig a trench or scrape a hole without disturbing the bones of his friends.

In 1918 came a downward curve, as to mere loathsomeness, since retreating and advancing, however sanguinary, were both a change.

Frenchmen at war—of Captain de Brisoult, Sergeant Bréjard, and Hutin, the layer of the gun, to mention only three—is one for which any country would be grateful.

Ma Pièce, besides being a careful narrative of facts, is part epic, part dirge. Though its author was anything but a lover of war, and was on the contrary from the very beginning singularly free from delusions on the subject, there is no very violent bitterness in it. Perhaps it was too early for that; the time for diatribes came later. He was, however, above all a conscientious realist; and one may venture to suppose that, if he had lived, he would have continued to see war steadily and whole, and would have remained content to set down the facts, leaving posterity to extract whatever message it could from them. Even had he shared the notion which seems to have taken root in the minds of M. Barbusse, Herr Remarque and others, that the world can be persuaded by books to abolish war for ever (because of its un-picnic-like character), he would probably have considered truth more eloquent when merely stripped bare than when tortured and lacerated almost beyond recognition into the bargain.[1] But there is a passage in his later journal which indicates what he felt in this connection at the time. The passage is dated in January 1916, when his battery was relieved after a particularly stormy tour of duty in the forest of Wolskopf, in Alsace:

"On the way out of the line, lulled by the easy motion of my horse, I thought of the dark days we have just lived

[1] It is true that these authors were infantrymen, or wrote from the infantryman's point of view, and that the infantry, as Lintier himself clearly recognises, had all the worst of it. Still, few infantrymen even of the later phases of the war would accept *Le Feu* or *Im Westen Nichts Neues* as honest descriptions based on actual experience. Such books are written in a mood which too clearly suggests other ideals than the preservation of the exact truth.

through. I dreamed of the pleasure it would be to me—if it should be granted me to survive—to come back later to these hills on a calm pilgrimage of memories. But I told myself that the aspect of these places would inevitably prove deceitful. I should like to contemplate here all the tragedy of days past, so that the days of peace might glow the more brightly by contrast, and so that I might feel the more intensely the joy of being alive. But such emotions, certainly, would elude me. Between the dreadful corpses of the tall pines and beeches, which will never again be green, new shoots will emerge. The leaves, turning to mould, will fill up all the shell-holes. Living nature will refuse to let this mountain preserve the eternal evidence of the risks we have here endured. Useless, therefore, to return. . . .

"And pursuing the same train of thought, I told myself that the flow of fair days and serene years, which perhaps await us, will slowly efface the bitter memories of this war. Ah, if for us these visions of terror never faded, if by words we could retrace them to our children and the children of our grandchildren, never again would the world know war. Alas! the seasons, in human memories as in the forest of Wolskopf, will cause new leaves to be put forth, and men's experience, once more, will bring no profit to men."

From which it appears that even so powerful a writer as Lintier put small faith in the lasting influence of words. Perhaps he was a pessimist unduly. . . . Possibly, again, in the long run, forgetfulness even of wars is a necessary part of the universal scheme. Be that as it may, the change which he foresaw has already operated on the battle-fields. Those who return can still, it is true, find their way here and there; but in order to be sure that they stand on some once familiar spot, they need a large scale map, considerably out of date, and the clearest of memories by which to read it. And, of course, when they are properly orientated, it is not the same. The essential beastliness has departed; the stink, the dirt, the sprawling, shattered deadness of things, the fear, the intimate, vile details—these exist only in the mind's eye of the pilgrim, and the altered landscape, even to him, is melancholy rather than sinister. The great stone cemeteries alone, though they lack the poignancy of the wooden crosses of ten years ago, are permanent. Perhaps theirs is a lasting message, a warning that will always be obvious. Lintier voices the warning; and since there was clearly nothing rancorous in his fervent and noble patriotism, we may be sure he would have admitted its universal application, to friend and foe alike.

"The plain is powdered with them," he wrote of the crosses, after the burial of a comrade killed in the offensive of autumn 1915, in Champagne; "the plain is powdered with them as the sky with stars. They are as many as the constellations in a brilliant Eastern night. These graves are lustrous. Most splendid are the ones that bear no name, the ones on which you read, '36 men of the 44th Infantry,' or '16 French soldiers.'

"When you look up with an embracing gaze at all the lights of the sky, you forget that they have names. You see neither Betelgeuse, Aldebaran nor Sirius; you contemplate the sky. So shall you contemplate this heroic landscape.

"And whenever in the future people come here, and see the great, uniform gesture traced by the crosses on the ground, as the sun in his course projects their shadows, let them pause and comprehend the greatness of the sacrifice. That is the wish of our dead, and the wish of us who may be dead to-morrow."

PUBLISHER'S NOTE

An English translation (slightly expurgated) of *Ma Pièce* was published in 1917 with the title of *My Seventy-Five*, and met with the common fate of most war-books issued at that time. The present new and complete version has been made by P. D., with valuable assistance from M. Pierre Mollard, late of the French Artillery, and Captain H. E. R., formerly R.F.A.

CONTENTS

LIST OF ILLUSTRATIONS

(Reproduced from contemporary photographs and drawings)

(The above are reproduced from *L'Illustration* and other sources.)

N.B.—For a map showing the German advance in 1914 and the line after the Battle of the Marne, see end-papers at the beginning and end of the volume.

Diary of Main Events of the Campaign on the Western Front in 1914

August 1*st*: France, Belgium and Germany order general mobilisation.

2*nd*: Hostilities commence on French frontier. German troops enter Luxembourg. German ultimatum to Belgium.

3*rd*: Germany declares war on France. England orders general mobilisation.

4*th*: Germany declares war on Belgium. Hostilities commence on Belgian frontier. England declares war on Germany.

6*th*: General Battle of the Frontiers begins.

7*th*: Liège occupied by the Germans.

14*th*–20*th*: Battle of Lorraine (Morhange and Sarrebourg).

16*th*: Landing of the B.E.F. in France completed.

20*th*: Germans occupy Brussels.

22*nd*: Battles of Charleroi and the Ardennes (including Virton).

23*rd*: Battle of Mons.

24*th*: Retreat of the Allied Armies becomes general.

25*th*: Fall of Namur.

26*th*: Battle of Le Cateau.

27*th*: Capitulation of Longwy.

August *29th–30th:* Battle of Guise (or St Quentin). Evacuation of Arras. Fall of Sedan.

30th: Laon, La Fère and Roye occupied by the Germans.

31st: Amiens entered by German forces.

September *1st:* Soissons occupied by the Germans.

3rd: Reims occupied by the Germans.

4th–12th: Battle of Lorraine (Grand Couronné, Nancy).

5th: End of the retreat of the Allied Armies. Battle of the Ourcq. German forces reach Claye (10 miles from Paris).

6th: Capitulation of Maubeuge.

6th–11th: Battle of the Marne.

10th: Antwerp occupied by the Germans.

12th–21st: Battle of the Aisne.

12th: Capitulation of Lille.

13th: Soissons, Compiègne and Amiens re-occupied.

14th: Germans evacuate Reims.

22nd–26th: Battle of Picardy (Noyon, Péronne, Bapaume).

27th–October 10th: Battle of Artois (Lens, La Bassée, Armentières, Messines, Hazebrouck). Capitulation of Antwerp.

October *12th:* Zeebrugge and Ostende occupied by German forces.

19th–November 22nd: First Battle of Ypres. Battle of the Yser.

December *20th:* First Battle of Champagne begins.

MY SEVENTY-FIVE

PART I

MOBILISATION

SATURDAY, *August 1st.*

WAR! It's bound to come. We all know it. Everything points to it: only a madman could think otherwise. Yet somehow one's emotions are very little stirred; one scarcely believes. War, the great European war—the thing's an impossibility.

Why an impossibility?

Bloodshed, money, blood, more blood. . . . Besides, it has been said so often before that there would be war, yet peace prevailed. Peace will prevail now; Europe will never be turned into an armed camp simply because an Austrian arch-duke has been assassinated. And yet . . . what are we waiting for, minute after minute, nervous, idle, confined to barracks, unless for mobilisation orders? Reservist N.C.O.'s of all ages came into Le Mans yesterday evening; and to-day every train has brought more of them. They have nothing to do. One man in a wide-skirted brown corduroy coat has been standing at the window since réveillé, watching the gunners and horses pass back and forth across the barrack square. Every now and then he takes a flask from his pocket and swallows a mouthful of brandy.

I was lying at full length on my bed. Hutin, layer of No. 1 gun, and my particular pal, lounged on his bed next to me. With his knees up and his heels drawn back, he was smoking. I looked up at my equipment, which hung above my head. It was slightly askew, and I got up mechanically to put it straight.

"Hutin!"

"What?"

"Come and have a drink."

"Right!"

The barrack square was quieter than usual. There were no men to be seen bringing their teams back from exercise and unharnessing them over by the stables. One missed the familiar sound of officers and sergeants shouting the words of command at drill in the shade of the plane trees. In one corner a man on guard was greasing a gun; a driver, with both hands in his pockets and the reins over his arm, was leading his horse to water or to the forge. In the glare of the sun, against the wall of the remount stables, two or three fatigue-men were grooming animals in a listless, half-hearted fashion. The only real sign of activity was a line of men walking to and from the canteen, diagonally across the square, like a dark line of insects against the white gravel of a pathway. At the door of the canteen there was a crush of thirsty men. The heat was intense.

Still no news at midday. Everyone was waiting. Could it possibly be yet another false alarm?

There were no parades, and the men, in white fatigue-dress, wandered idly about the square in expectation of further news. A group of civilians came to press their faces against the bars of the closed gates, scarcely knowing what they expected to see. They were mostly women. Inside, some of the gunners marched up and down with an air, smiling, their caps tilted over one ear, seeing themselves already in the part of their country's defenders.

Near the guardhouse that serves for a parlour, but into which visitors are not admitted because of the fleas that swarm there at this time of year, wives, mothers, sisters and sweethearts had come to see their soldiers. They were all brave. They hid their emotion. But anxiety had sharpened their features and furrowed their brows, and they seemed to have aged. Their eyes were careworn and intense, and had dark rings round them. They glanced from side to side, as though afraid lest by a direct look they should betray the apprehension and fear that none of them could beat down. As they left, through the little door under the chestnut trees, after watching their men disappear down a passage into the barracks, their emotion broke out suddenly and irresistibly in a loud sob. Quickly, half ashamed, they crushed a handkerchief to their lips, and turned abruptly into the Rue Chanzy; as if all the men who saw them did not understand their sorrow . . .

At four o'clock I left barracks with Quartermaster-Sergeant Le Mée, having obtained special leave from the captain. We went to my room in the Rue Mangeard, to deposit his walking-out kit, some papers and a valise.

We sat down to dine. I had uncorked a bottle of old Bordeaux, when Le Mée grasped my arm.

"Listen!"

A loud murmur rose from the street through the open window. At the same instant something magnetic, not to be put into words, yet very definite, passed through each of us. We looked at each other across the table. . . . The bottle hung motionless over the rim of the glass.

"It's come!"

"Yes," nodded Le Mée, "it has come." We ran to the window. Down below in the street, moving towards the barracks, we saw a rolling wave of heads. Every face wore the same expression of blank stupor and distraction; in all the eyes was the same strange phosphorescent gleam. There came a hoarse, strangled sound of women's voices.

"Well, Le Mée, here's health to you. And may we crack a bottle again together a few months hence."

"Here's to us!"

And picking up our swords we ran back to barracks. It was to be our last night in bed.

SUNDAY, *August 2nd.*

My haversack was ready and I had rolled up some handkerchiefs in my greatcoat, when a non-commissioned officer came into the room.

"Fall in outside the orderly-room!"

The sergeant-major was issuing pay-books and identity discs.

Mine had on one side *Lintier, Paul,* with, below, *E.V.*[1] *Cl. 1913*; and on the other, *Mayenne, 1179*.

Inside the orderly-room you could have heard the beat of a fly's wings. I had a momentary vision of a battlefield, with a heap of dead bodies by the side of a ditch, and an officer identifying them before they were buried. It was only the briefest of sensations. . . .

More than anything else, the Great Event has interrupted the monotony of barrack life. A strange sort of blindness seems to prevent us from visualising the future that lurks behind our preparations for departure. This carelessness astonishes me, but I share it myself.

Is it resolution, courage? Hardly, I think, or only to a very small extent. . . . Do we really believe that this is war? I am not sure. It is impossible to imagine what war means or to foresee its horrors. It gives us no qualms.

[1] *Engagé volontaire.*

Seen from a barrack window. The man, quite young, called up at once on mobilisation, had just left the threshold of his home, and was walking backwards, shading his eyes with his hands, in the endeavour to catch a last glimpse against the sun of a loved face at a second-floor window immediately above him. She, fair, very young too, and deadly pale, was watching him through the muslin curtains, being doubtless afraid to let him see her stricken face and eyes swimming with tears. She stood close to the curtain with her fingers spread across her breast, in a tragically mournful attitude. Just as he was on the point of passing out of sight round a corner, she suddenly flung the window wide open and showed herself for an instant. The man could not have seen her. Then she took two faltering steps back into the room and sank nervelessly into a chair, her face buried in her hands, her whole frame shaken with sobbing. In the half-light I saw a nurse, wearing a Breton cap, bring a tiny baby to her.

At noon we left barracks for the billets allotted us on mobilisation. A short march along the Avenue de Pontlieue, and we were there.

The Toublanc cider brewery is to be the scene of the formation on a war footing of the 10th and 11th Batteries of the 44th Regiment of Field Artillery.

We have nothing to do, meanwhile, except to put down straw for bedding. A gas-engine somewhere in the building makes an incessant thud, thud, exasperating in its monotony. . . . The distributions of men are chalked up roughly on the doors of the various parts of the brewery taken over as billets.

The teams are stabled in an open shed, and the harness is heaped on a row of barrels at the back of it. The quarters would be excellent but for the close proximity of some primitive latrines that stink abominably.

The men are installed at one end of an orchard of black-currant and peach trees, in a hovel that only seems to be kept from falling to bits by the intertwined vines and ivy that cling to its decrepit walls. The grapes are already large. There will be a fine harvest. . . . Where shall we be at the vintage-time?

One scarcely worries about knowing if war has been declared, if the few words have actually been pronounced or are about to be pronounced by diplomats. The war is already a reality. We feel it. When do we march? That is the one question that fills our minds. No one can answer it.

The men are gay, light-hearted, much less nervous than yesterday. Nor do I myself feel that vast load of anxiety weighing on my mind which I should have expected at such a moment. I should like to ask all my comrades: "Do you look forward with all your heart to being in action in a few days' time?" And if they answered "Yes," I should admire them; for if I am calm enough myself on the edge of the abyss, it is only that my imagination has not yet sounded its depths.

I say over and over again to myself: "This is war, ghastly, bloody war; perhaps death for me in a day or two." And I feel no emotion. I can't believe in it. Similarly, before the dead body of someone much loved, one cannot at first believe in death.

Seated on a wooden box, I am writing these notes with a cask for table. The man on stable-guard, who has been watching me for the last minute or two, has just looked over my shoulder.

"Nom d'un chien!" he says; "you're a cheerful devil, I must say!"

MONDAY, *August 3rd.*

We still do not know this morning if war has been declared, but they say Metz is in flames, and some even say it has fallen. French aeroplanes and dirigibles, according to the story, have bombed the powder-magazines. They say Garros has destroyed a Zeppelin manned by twenty officers. They say our aviators at the frontier draw lots as to who shall be the first to attack the enemy's airships. They say the Germans crossed the frontier yesterday at three places. But it was reported yesterday that our own troops, against their officers' orders, had entered German territory. They say . . . they say . . . they say the wisest and silliest things equally.

What is one to believe? Evidently, nothing; which would be the best of all.

But we wait all the time for news. When any comes, there is shrugging of shoulders; though when it is news of success, such is our anxiety to believe it that the majority of us, even the most sceptical, only require a sufficiently emphatic assertion to be convinced. I want to set down fables as well as history day by day. And indeed at the present time I am not in a position to distinguish the true from the false.

I only aim at putting on record, in these hastily written leaves, the various things that combine to create the state of mind of a soldier lost in the crowd of soldiers. In this sense, fable and truth are all one. But later, unless my pocket-book goes down with me into the "hole" somewhere at the front, these notes may perhaps serve for a history of the legend. A history of the legend: a world theme!

I have leisure to write again. A bench does duty as my desk. From behind me comes the irregular clatter of the horses' hoofs stamping on the cement floor of their shed. I should do very well here; but how those latrines stink! . . .

They say we move on Friday. *A Berlin!* To Berlin! Berlin is the objective. It is on everyone's lips. But—was not that the very refrain to which heels were tapping forty-four years ago, at almost the same season of the year? And what an awakening came after! The thought fills me with horror. Prejudice!

Will England take the field by our side against Germany? England is the great unknown for the moment, though very little is said of it here.

To Berlin! To Berlin!

One hears nothing else.

I am beginning to be convinced of the reality of what is taking place. But the excitement of departure, and the irritation of not knowing anything for certain, already affects one's nerves with a sort of feverish activity that prevents one from fully realising the horror that is imminent.

We have paired off our horses and made up the gun-teams. The unit in a 75 mm. battery consists, in material, of a gun-limber and ammunition-waggon, each drawn by a team of six horses harnessed in pairs; and, in personnel, of six drivers, six gunners, a corporal, and a sergeant in command. But my own gun, No. 1 of the 11th Battery, also includes the section-sergeant, a fire-corporal, a trumpeter and the captain's groom with his two horses: in all, eighteen men and nineteen animals. Of the eighteen men, seventeen are serving soldiers on the active list. For almost a year they have lived the same life and drilled or manœuvred together every day. Thus the gun's crew has a separate existence; it forms a microcosm, with its own friendships, antipathies and habits.

As things now are, Bréjard, the section-sergeant, commands the gun for all practical purposes, as he did before mobilisation. There is no apparent change.

Hubert, the new sergeant in command of the gun, has been called up from the reserve, and can think of nothing at the moment but his young wife, from whom he has had to part after only a few months of married life, and his farm, which he has left with the harvest still ungathered.

Sergeant Bréjard is twenty-four years old; tall, thin and fair, with steady grey eyes, a determined chin and an open, frank expression. He enlisted very young, and recently, as a result of consistent hard work and good conduct, won a first-class nomination to the military academy at Fontainebleau.

Corporal Jean Déprez is in direct contrast with Bréjard. Déprez is a dreamer; barrack life bores him, nor is he much cheered by the prospect of long months of active service. There is nothing of the martinet about Déprez, and indeed he finds the exercise of his authority, however trivial the occasion, irksome. Witty by fits and starts, usually indifferent, inclined to be moody, but a congenial talker when he chooses and a sure friend, he and I have been drawn together in the last few months during the long hours off duty, and we are glad to be taking the field together now.

Between my corporal and Hutin, the gun-layer, I have no feeling of loneliness in the midst of the mighty rumblings of mobilisation, before the bursting of the storm.

Hutin is a little dark man, with a thick crop of hair and heavy moustaches. Fine dark eyes, with a sardonic twinkle in them, light up his regular features. His temperament is ardent and impulsive; he is energetic, downright, ambitious, easily provoked, quick to make decisions, and perhaps more than anything else, intelligent; and I have a great affection for him.

The requisitioned horses have been drawn up for inspection under the plane trees in the Avenue de Pontlieue: hundreds of placid, big-bellied beasts with flowing manes and bushy fetlocks, in charge of men in blue smocks who stand motionless along the edge of the sidewalk, hungry and bored with waiting. Near by, along the wall of the artillery barracks, are numbers of requisitioned carts and waggons, left standing anyhow as the horses were taken out of the shafts.

A motley crowd of women in light summer dresses, soldiers in uniform or fatigue-dress, and others wearing ludicrous mixtures of uniform and civilian clothes, is walking up and down the middle of the street. Little groups of reservists arrive from time to time. Most of them are perfectly calm; one or two are merry, a few are drunk, and some seem as if they were. I have only seen one in tears. He was sitting on a truss of hay, fastening a clean new strap to his revolver-holster. Tears were dropping on to his fumbling fingers. I laid a hand on his shoulder, and he looked up and nodded miserably.

"Oh God! My wife died just a week ago to-day, giving birth to a child. . . . A week-old baby, and no one to look after it. . . ."

"What did you do?"

"What else was there but to take it to the workhouse?"

It is when the post arrives that faces are saddest.

Late in the afternoon we were confined to our billets;

but the N.C.O.'s are allowed to take parties of men "to water" at the café opposite.

TUESDAY, *August 4th.*

At nine o'clock last night the lieutenant made an informal inspection of the billets. He put his head in at the door of our shed:

"All right in there?"

"Yes, mon lieutenant; warm as little rabbits!"

"Nothing you want?"

"Nothing at all, sir, except to get a move on."

This morning Pelletier, the trumpeter, a Parisian and a complete handy-man, undertook to sharpen all our swords. Leaning over a bench in his shirt-sleeves, he manipulated an enormous file with a horrible grating noise that sent a shiver down one's back and gave one goose-flesh. Every now and then he dropped the file and, by way of testing the points and edges, lunged and slashed furiously at some empty deal packing-cases in a corner of the room.

Inside our billet, where we live in the midst of the wildest rumours, waiting for the order to entrain, and outside in the streets and on the Paris-Brest railway line close by, the general mobilisation seems one continuous roar of thunder in an atmosphere saturated with electricity.

Gaget, a headquarters clerk, who comes from my native place, told me just now that war has not been declared yet. He is well placed to know the truth. He has had a letter from his mother at Mayenne, in which she says that my family think I am at Verdun already. Do my letters not reach home then?

Déprez went to the laundry to fetch his clean linen. A young woman in the shop, whose husband, a corporal in the artillery, left for the Front this morning, fell on his neck and burst into tears.

He came back deeply moved.

A fatigue-party has been sent with a waggon to the docks to collect our war material. The guns are parked along the broad sidewalk of the Avenue de Pontlieue, under the plane trees. Two sentries with fixed bayonets are on guard. Women stop from time to time as they go by, and look at the battery. Some of them shake their heads.

It seems we are to entrain to-morrow evening.

We are beginning to be bored here; we don't know how to occupy the time. I am going to turn in for a sleep in our shed at the end of the garden, where it is dark and cool. The evening sun, through the open door, gilds one large square of straw, on which are nosebags and gleaming arms. It has been a perfect day, clear, pure and luminous, and the air is beginning to fill with whirling swarms of midges, an indication of more fine weather to come.

I was able to get out for a brief spell. The women, red-eyed, enveloped us with tenderness by look, voice and gesture—us in particular, the youngest, who will be the first to go.

"When do you leave?"

"To-morrow . . . or the day after. . . ."

"Where for?"

"Verdun, most likely, or Maubeuge. . . ."

"Well, good luck to you!"

Always good luck. They wish us good luck with all their hearts, as a viaticum for the unknown.

"Thanks!"

WEDNESDAY, *August 5th.*

War has been declared since August 3rd. Fighting is in progress all along the frontier.

Appalling casualties are announced already: eleven thousand French and eighteen thousand Germans are said to have fallen in the opening battles. Can this refer to killed alone or does it include losses of all sorts?

Whether true or not, the news shook us considerably for a moment. But almost at once our extraordinary carelessness reasserted itself, to the exclusion of every other feeling. And besides, was there ever a more favourable time for the *revanche*?

THURSDAY, *August 6th.*

The Germans have entered Belgium, in spite of the treaty of neutrality. I don't think this surprises anyone. But what does astonish us, and what must amaze the enemy, is the magnificent resistance offered by the Belgians. A mass attack launched by the Germans against Liège has completely failed. If the Belgian Army alone has been able to stand against them, what may we not hope for?

England is with us. That is certain now. With the French, English, Russians, Belgians and Serbs united, we shall soon see the end of the military power that has been called so formidable. This news, which is really official this time, has made us more than ever eager to leave Le Mans and have done with waiting.

Train-loads of infantry, cavalry and supplies are going by almost incessantly along the Paris-Brest line. Slowly, and with much clanking, they cross the bridge over the Avenue de Pontlieue, which is guarded by heroic, pot-bellied Territorials armed with old Gras rifles and wearing any sort of uniform. Crowds of women, with infants in their arms or clinging to their skirts, wait below in the blazing sun. They have stood there for hours on end, watching the endless procession of military trains all festooned with leaves and decorated with crude chalk drawings. There are clusters of soldiers on the footboards and in the brake-cabins and guards' vans.

Some requisitioned horses which were being harnessed and made up into waggon-teams in the roadway began kicking and struggling, and finally got entangled in the traces, raising clouds of dust. The women hastily scattered, dragging their children beyond reach of the trampling hoofs and waggon-wheels. Then at once, in the fervour of their obsession, and as though drunk with the movement, light and noise, they resumed their vigil, and are keeping to it in spite of everything. And as each train goes by, a strangely loud chorus of shrill cries rises from the various groups that are formed, broken up, dispersed and huddled together by the succeeding hazards of the traffic.

Outside the gates of the Toublanc cider brewery the guns and waggons and all the sidewalk are covered with bunches of flowers and festoons and streamers of ribbon. Women and girls have been bringing armfuls of hortensias, gladioluses and roses; their faces, animated by the sun and the emotion of the hour, their bright eyes and smooth, glistening hair appear from the midst of a framework of flowers. As the sentry has orders to let no one approach, they have to throw their bouquets from a distance. The fatigue-men, having finished loading up the waggons, blow them kisses by way of thanks with a heartiness that puts them to instant flight.

The young fiancée of one of the sentries has just stuck a great tricolour bunch on the end of his bayonet. The bright steel gleams among the flowers.

Women stop the mounted men as they pass to put flowers in their bridles and saddle-buckles. And all the scene is bathed in the clear August sunlight, which shines on the dust, the green trees, the women's faces and the flowers.

FRIDAY, *August 7th.*

I have long since discovered what a soldier's first movement is when he gets a letter. He tears it open, and without taking it out of the envelope, eagerly feels to see whether it contains a note or a postal order.

While I was walking out this evening with Déprez, a blowzy woman of the town, whose breast and stomach merged in a trembling mass of fat, accosted us in the street:

"44th?"

"Yes."

"Do you know Corporal X . . .? Wish him good luck from Alice, will you? He'll know. Alice. You won't forget. . . . Poor Jojo!"

Then, as we were moving on:

"Won't you come along with me?" she asked, with the customary leer.

Very politely Déprez answered:

"No, thanks. We haven't the time."

And when we had walked a few steps farther he added:

"I don't propose to deliver *that* message."

SATURDAY, *August 8th.*

At last we're off.

The war began, for us, with a fête of flowers. A crowd of women and grey-headed men stood waiting under the plane trees on the far side of the avenue. Children came over to us with their arms full of flowers. Their mothers, who sent them, were smiling; but how sad, how heart-broken were those women's smiles! . . . Their swollen eyelids showed that they had been crying, and it was easy to see by their trembling lips that the tears were still very close behind their smiles. But for the children—and the tiniest infants came to us across the street—to-day was better than a fair. They crowed and shouted with merriment.

We had spent the earlier part of the morning getting our vehicles ready and harnessing in the horses. Towards noon, as the hour of departure drew near, the noise and bustle in the avenue decreased. The crowd stood motionless in the shade of the trees, waiting, like ourselves. . . .

The silence was almost absolute when the captain gave the word of command in clear, full, resonant tones:

"En avant!"

A great cheer rose like an echo from the crowd—a cheer that included, very distinctly, two heart-rending sobs.

Never was August day more luminous. The rails of the limbers, the wheels, the hooks and buckles of the harness, even the muzzles of the guns were decked with ribbons and flowers, the gay colours of which blended into a bright blaze against the grey paint of the battery.

Our officer, Captain Bernard de Brisoult, had said to us earlier in the day:

"Take the flowers that are offered you, and adorn your guns with them. They are a precious parting gift from the women we are leaving behind us. But be calm, for so you will give them the most confidence when they watch you go."

The streets being cobbled, we moved off at a walk. And there was something in the serene bearing of the men, many of whom will doubtless never return, that compelled admiration. The gunners smiled, as they sat motionless on the limbers or yielded to the quiet motion of the walking horses. The women who lined the streets waved to us with tragic gestures; and we were deeply moved. But it was their emotion, the general emotion of the people, that affected us rather than any inner feelings of our own.

The business of entraining at the station was simple. The men hoisted their vehicles on to the open trucks. It was a hot afternoon; they took off their coats and, with red faces and shoulders to the wheel, shoved together on the word, "*Oh, ferme!*" given by the section-commanders and monotonously repeated in an interminable echo all along the platform. Getting the animals into the vans was not so easy. The old battery horses knew the manœuvre, but the requisitioned ones were restive and resisted. One had to pass a surcingle round their quarters and so force them up the gangways. Once in the van, they had still to be turned and closed together so as to make room for four aside. The beasts being finally installed, and kept in place by means of breast-ropes, the harness and forage for the journey were stacked by the stable-guards in the space between the two rows of horses.

When the train started I felt momentarily dazed. Something seemed to break inside my chest, and a sort of anguish choked me. Shall I come back? Yes, yes! I am sure I shall. But why am I so sure? . . .

Connéré-Beillé. I am sitting on a truss of hay between my eight horses. They continually make snatches at the fodder and shift my seat, despite my whip. The door of the van is wide open to the sun-drenched landscape.

SUNDAY, *August 9th.*

We have been on the move for fifteen or eighteen hours. I am on stable-guard, which is the least uncomfortable position to be in on a journey of this kind. I shook out my truss of hay and had a good sleep in it, with my head well ensconced between the stuffed sides of an upturned saddle.

It was already daylight when the horses, which are almost all affected with strangles, woke me up by sneezing and slobbering on my face. A thick summer mist still lingers in the fields to about a man's height, and the sun, piercing it in places, makes the dew on the grass sparkle marvellously.

The gunners, sitting at the open doors of the trucks with their feet dangling, watch the countryside go by. When an empty train rushes past us the scared horses neigh loudly. Where are we making for? Our officers themselves don't know, and the engine-driver declares he doesn't know either. He says he is to get his orders on the way.

The Territorials on guard along the line raise their rifles at arm's length above their heads to salute us as we pass, and we crack our whips in response.

"Good morning, old 'uns!"

"Good luck, young 'uns!"

Reims. A fleeting glimpse of the canal and wharves, then a wide, luminous landscape, covered with ripe corn. In a few fields it has just been cut and gathered into sheaves; but almost everywhere it is still standing, motionless in the heat, gilding the slow hills and the serene, majestic movement of the lovely landscape.

I must open my eyes wide. It may be that in a few days I shall see no more the beauty of the corn in the sunshine, the grave contours of the earth swelling beneath its sumptuous gold cloak, like some lovely figure veiled in the clinging mantle of old Greece.

We are going to Verdun. As the train rolls slowly onward, in every village, in each garden along the line, at every level crossing, children and young girls blow kisses to us. They throw flowers and, when the convoy halts, bring us refreshing drink.

In the twilight, after passing the interminable platforms of Verdun, on which great military bakehouses had been installed under green canvas awnings, the train at last came to a stop at Charny. We had been travelling for more than thirty hours. Night came on as we detrained.

PART II

THE MARCH TO THE FRONTIER

THE sun had set when we crossed the Meuse; but the west was red still, and the river, between the marshy islands in the middle and the reed-beds by the banks, seemed flowing blood. To-morrow, I thought, or the next day, blood may flow there really. In the doubtful moment of late dusk I was strangely moved by the blood-red reflections in the waters of the Meuse.

In the clear night sky I looked uneasily among the stars for the beams of searchlights. . . . By the side of the road, in a military cage for live-stock, we passed an innumerable sleeping herd of beasts. All the landscape was utterly still and quiet except for the low rumble of our column on the march. The last echoes of day and the first pale glimmer of the moon, from below the eastern horizon, mingled together in a curious, diffuse half-light.

We were marching east; and, as the road rounded the dark mass of a high hill, the moon appeared before us, delineating tall silhouettes of fir trees against the sky. Soon afterwards the battery entered a sombre woodland in which it was hard to see the road. No one talked. From time to time, through a clearing between the trees, the moon suddenly shone out on the figure of a man on horseback, powdering him, as it were, with a dust of yellow light. There were quick glints of polished metal. Then he disappeared, his place being taken by others in succession. Their clear-cut shadows on the road seemed to form part of their silhouettes, magnifying them enormously. Of the rest of the long column, lost in the night of the forest, nothing was visible.

We had been told that the enemy was not far off, somewhere in the plain beyond the hills; and at every cross-roads we were nervous lest a mistake should lead us into the German lines. And there was something fantastic, too, about this, our first night march of the war, that worked powerfully on our imaginations.

The column halted on the outskirts of a village. Other troops were already encamped on either side of the road, and in a field below one made out vague outlines of parked guns or supply-waggons. The air, despite the late hour, was quite warm. A thin mist veiled the brilliance of the stars. Bare-chested soldiers, some naked from the waist up, stood out from the surrounding blackness in the glare of bivouac fires.

A little farther on, in a dewy meadow where the men and beasts of the 10th Battery were already asleep, we formed our park.

With the bare ground to lie on, a struggle of wits ensued for possession of the horse-rugs. Most of the men crawled under the guns or limbers, where the dampness of the night was less penetrating. It fell to me, being still on stable-guard, to attend to the horses, which were fastened side by side to a rope stretched between two pickets. They were restless and bit one another; the head collars of several were loose, and they shook them off and ran away into the darkness. My night was passed in mad chasings after them. One in particular, a little black horse, eluded capture for more than an hour; and I only caught him, in the end, by rattling some grains of fodder in the bottom of a nosebag.

Whip in hand and soaked with dew up to the knees, I felt I was playing my part most conscientiously.

MONDAY, *August 10th.*

Three in the morning. The grey shadow of an airship slid across the stars. Was it friend or foe?

At the first hint of dawn the camp came to life. The men emerged, draped in their coverings, from between the wheels and under the limbers, and shook and stretched themselves.

Holes were scraped for fires, and wood and water collected, and very soon mess-tins were filled with steaming coffee.

Line regiments began to move off along the road from Verdun, with the expectation of being in action quite shortly. The long red and blue column undulated with the sinuous movements of a crawling beast. Very soon the houses and trees of the village hid the battalions; but farther off, scarcely perceptible in the distance, one could just make out the undulation of troops marching along the thin white road up a gilded hillside. We expected the order to harness up at any moment.

Imagine us encamped in a meadow bounded on one side by a marsh, through which a mill-stream flows between tall grass, and on the other by a long, gently sloping field where the corn has been cut and stacked in sheaves. To the east a high hill, its sides covered with symmetrical strips of yellow barley and tawny wheat, seems a mountain of gold in the sun.

Behind the parallel lines of our picketed horses the harness makes dark patches against the grass. We are lying there on horse-rugs and ground-sheets; saddles, balanced on the pommels, shade the heads of a row of sleeping gunners, care-free, half undressed, with bellies bare to the sun.

I should have slept well myself after the tiring exploits of the night, but I kept thinking of the terrible anxiety which must be felt by those I have left at home at the news of the slaughter in Alsace. They don't know where I am. Wherever there is fighting, there, for all they know, I may be.

On the road columns of artillery succeeded the line regiments. By nine o'clock there was still no sound to indicate a battle.

A driver shook out his horse-rug noisily. It made me jump, and Déprez, who was sleeping beside me, woke up with a start. Gun-fire? No, not yet. . . .

The army of Alsace is at Mulhouse. There has been a great battle at Altkirch, and we are the victors. The news is official. It is the beginning of the revanche. But they talk of fifty thousand dead!

The spectacle of the high golden hills to the east, behind which lay our destiny, held Déprez and me with a kind of magnetic fascination. We realised that there were men over there, masses of men in the plains and the woods, who would kill us unless we killed them.

In the overpowering heat these thoughts wandered through my mind, and especially that horror of fifty thousand dead, scattered over the plains of Alsace. Finally I fell asleep. . . .

The report of a revolver roused me. A horse which had broken a leg had been shot. It is going to be cut up, and the best pieces distributed through the battery.

We shall not be engaged to-day. It has been decided to make soup for dinner, and the men are building straw shelters for the night in the field where the sheaves of corn are.

At dusk a dank mist rose from the marsh and the stream The night was fine. Déprez and I, booted and spurred, with our revolver-holsters within reach, went to sleep side by side on a bed of straw with our faces to the stars, which are brighter here than we have been accustomed to see them at home.

TUESDAY, *August 11th.*

We have been standing by to move since daylight.

Some men of the 130th Regiment of the Line have come into billets in the village, which is called Ville-devant-Chaumont. While waiting for our marching orders I entered into conversation with a little ruddy-faced sergeant, rather like a cat in appearance.

"Ah," he said, "you're from Mayenne, are you? . . . Well, I don't know how many of the 130th will ever see Mayenne again. . . . The regiment was in action yesterday, and the casualties were heavy, I can tell you! My own battalion was out of it, but the other two . . . there are companies down to ten men and no officers. It's their machine-guns that do it. . . . But what can you expect, with two battalions against a division!"

"But why couldn't they at least use all three battalions of the regiment?"

"*I* don't know. . . . No one knows anything at the front."

And he added:

"There were some fine efforts all the same. Lieutenant X, for example: he got up, drew his sword, and unbuttoned his tunic at the neck, then he shouted, 'Charge, my lads!' and fell dead. . . . And the colours. . . . They were taken by the enemy, recaptured by a major, lost again, and then in the end one of the men, a private, got hold of them, and went and hid them under a bridge just before he was killed. A section of the 115th found them there later. . . . And then the gunners came along at last—three batteries of the 31st. Cleaned 'em up in no time. They left two batteries on the field. . . ."

Orders came to unharness. The heat was tremendous, and a mirage rose from the ground, making the distance shimmer. From time to time a dull sound of cannonading could be heard, but more often the rumble of vehicles on the road gave one the illusion of it. Little white clouds formed on the hilltops, and looked so like puffs of smoke from bursting shells that one was quite deceived for a moment.

A soldier of the 130th arrived from the battlefield in a lamentable state, without cap, equipment or arms. How he had dragged himself so far was a mystery. His eyes stared wildly. The gunners gathered round him; but he, all huddled up and with his head lolling from side to side, only answered their questions with a wide sweep of his arm, muttering:

"Mown down! Ah! . . . Mown down!"

His voice sank to a whisper and then failed altogether; but his lips went on framing the words:

"Mown down! . . . Mown down!"

And he collapsed on the ground in the middle of us and suddenly fell fast asleep, with his mouth wide open and misery in his face. Two of the gunners carried him into a barn close by.

A priest of Ville-devant-Chaumont is said to have been arrested and taken to Verdun under suspicion of being a spy.

The unexpected leisure gave us the chance to wash our linen and bathe in the stream. Afterwards we spread out our drawers, socks and shirts to dry in the sun and sat naked on the grass, talking.

WEDNESDAY, *August 12th.*

Frenchmen love a heroic legend. I have now learnt the truth about the action in which two battalions of the

130th were cut to pieces; and it in no way resembles the epic story told by the little fair-haired sergeant with the face like a cat.

On August 10th the officers of the 130th were quite unaware of the enemy's presence in their neighbourhood, and a party of men were taken by surprise on their way to wash, being unarmed and only half dressed. Thereupon a battle started, and the 130th was soon fighting hard against superior odds, without receiving any support, at least at the beginning of the action, from the artillery, which in the absence of any orders stayed in its billets. But eventually three batteries of the 31st arrived and broke up the German attack. The ground remained in our possession.

As for Lieutenant X, who according to the story had met his death with bared breast, leading his men to the charge; what really happened was that he fell into a deep stream called the Loison. The shock of the fall and the coldness of the water, together with the excitement of being in action for the first time, brought on an attack of congestion. He is perfectly fit again now; which is fortunate, for Lieutenant X is an excellent officer.

A number of the men, having charged in too much of a hurry, also fell into the stream, which flows through long grass between very low banks. They stayed where they were, as well protected as if they had been in a trench, and fought on. The colours of the 130th, on August 10th, never emerged from their oilcloth sheath.

The whole of to-day has been devoted to washing, cooking and long spells of sleep. Several of the waggons were detailed to carry wounded men of the 130th to Verdun.

Before turning in for the night we have been singing choruses, lying on spread corn-sheaves under the clear sky.

I wish our people at home who are so anxiously waiting for news of us could see us now.

THURSDAY, *August 13th.*

Some men of the 130th brought back a grey German overcoat, a pair of boots, a uhlan's helmet, and a kind of round infantryman's cap like a small cheese. These spoils of war, hung up in a barn, attracted a crowd of gunners. They belonged to a sergeant-major, who showed them to the visitors, and drew particular attention to a little rent in the back of the overcoat.

"That's the hole that killed him," he said. "Steinberg was his name; it's stamped on the inside. Look!"

And he threw out his chest proudly.

The inaction and the heat are weighing on us equally. We want to fight, and at the same time we are a little nervous.

As I write, we are most of us lying in the shade of horse-rugs and ground-sheets stretched between pickets.

Monday's action will be known as the affair at Mangiennes.

FRIDAY, *August 14th.*

We harnessed and hooked in at dawn, waiting for orders. The commanding officer moved the battery forward on to a narrow road leading into the main Verdun highway. We drew in to the right, and the horses stood pawing and splashing in a little stream that came out of a pond farther up. Meanwhile the sun rose in the heavens. No orders came for us, so we unbridled the animals and gave them a feed.

The reserve regiments of the Army Corps began to file past us along the left of the road: the 301st, 303rd and 330th. Their trousers were white with dust up to the knees, their faces grimy and stiff with a week's growth of stubbly beard. Their greatcoats were open at the neck and folded back under the straps of their equipment; here and there one saw a hairy chest. The weight of their packs made the muscles of their necks stand out. These men were reservists, and had a serious, determined, grim look about them.

They went by in a solid mass, with a noise like that of a torrent pouring over loose pebbles. At the sight of our guns their faces lit up with satisfied smiles. Battalion after battalion climbed the hill in front of us; there were so many men that one saw neither the road nor the red of their trousers. There was a ceaseless twinkle all along the moving ribbon from the mess-tins and picks and shovels on the men's backs.

We filled our canvas buckets with fresh water, and as the infantrymen came by they dipped their tin cups in and marched on, cup to lip, diminishing the undulation of their walk so as to lose none of the precious liquid.

At last the battery moved off, but only, so we were told, to go into new billets at Azannes, four or five kilometres to the south-east of Ville-devant-Chaumont, where we should be hardly any nearer to the enemy.

On the main road cars full of senior officers, troops of chasseurs escorting gold-braided staffs, motor-lorries and our own vehicles raised a continuous cloud of dust. Our dark uniforms turned suddenly grey. The dust clung to our hair, eyebrows and beards, and by the time a column of Paris motor-buses, transformed into meat-lorries, had gone by us, we were as white as the road itself.

"Reconnaissance!"

"What?"

"Reconnaissance—pass the word!"

The corporals repeated the order down the column. Our captain, spurring his horse forward, said simply:

"We're coming into action."

The commanding officer, the captains of the three batteries, and the trumpeters and fire-corporals collected into a little group and at once rode off at a gallop.

We went on through Azannes, where we had expected to go into billets: a wretched-looking village, chiefly remarkable for dunghills. It is obvious that man has never dared to undertake much constructive work hereabouts. Not that the land is poor, but the perpetual threat of war and invasion has curbed all initiative. To be poor is to have less to lose.

Beyond Azannes the column relapsed into silence. The road ran by the side of a cemetery. Its walls had been battlemented by the infantry, and through occasional loopholes one caught a glimpse of gravestones, shrines and crosses. Powdered mortar and bits of broken stone lay in the gutter along the foot of the wall. Farther on, in a field by the edge of a wood, some digging had been done; a narrow trench, with leafy branches spread along it which were already turning brown, made a great scar of bright red ochre against the rich green of the grass.

There were strands of barbed wire in front of the trench, so that we knew the enemy could not be far away.

As the column rolled steadily forward one had time to examine one's sensations; and I found that this waiting for my first experience of battle engendered an acute and undeniable nervousness. Great woods extended on either side of us: the contrast was startling and uncanny between the road, made dazzling white by the midday sun, and the dark forest, through which narrow, arched glades opened long perspectives of dizzy verdure. What grim struggle of surprise and ambush might not be going on in those depths between uhlan and chasseur!

We passed a horse standing in the ditch by the side of the road, with its head hanging down. Viscous threads of slaver depended from its nostrils. It never stirred at the clatter of our column. One wondered that the bony structure of its quarters had not come through the skin; its flanks, expanding and contracting in quick, short breaths, seemed drawn together behind the ribs, as though emptied of flesh and entrails. The sight of the poor beast was acutely painful. In the dim light of a glade another abandoned horse was still browsing.

Between two woods, as we advanced, a lake gleamed, fringed with reeds and bulrushes. The dark mass of greenery in the middle distance enhanced the brilliance of its silvery, mirror-like surface; beyond, the high and noble hills that had shut in our horizon from Ville-devant-Chaumont, and which we had now rounded, formed a lovely blue-grey background for the water. A farmhouse stood near the road. And in a little meadow near the sluice of the lake, in the shade of an elder bush, there was a recently dug grave. A cross, made of two branches nailed together, had been planted in the newly turned earth; and a page had been torn from a square-ruled notebook and stuck on a projecting twig, with a name written on it in pencil.

Farther on, coming to the end of the forest, our batteries rapidly deployed along the side of a broad valley; the guns half disappeared in tall standing corn, in which the presence of a number of invisible infantrymen was only revealed by occasional rufflings of the surface, like cat's-paws of wind on an expanse of still water.

Where was the enemy? How good was our position, and could it be overlooked? Was there any infantry covering us in front? With such self-questionings, for we were highly nervous and excited, we formed up in a meadow at the edge of the cornfield. The teams and waggons withdrew to the rear and took cover in the wood, and Bréjard lost no time in making us dig up sods of earth with which to reinforce the protection afforded by the gun shields.

All that one saw, looking out towards the front, was the motionless corn, like a vast expanse of molten metal, and the blue summer sky. The layer could find neither tree nor other prominent object by which to lay the gun, and a shovel had to be stuck in the ground in front. One would have had no inkling of the great force of artillery waiting for the enemy in that field—more than sixty guns—had one not seen them moving into position. Except for the observation-ladders from which the captains in command of the batteries were surveying the country to the north-east, like great black insects on the end of long stalks, there was nothing to be seen.

In a very short time we were ready to fire, and lay down in rear of the guns to await developments. No sound of battle was to be heard. Then an orderly officer rode up to the major with a message. The captain, taking off his cap and waving it from side to side, signalled to the waggons and teams to come up.

"What now?"

"We're going to move," said Bréjard, who had overheard the orders.

"Are the Germans not there?"

"I don't know. The officer said that from now on the 4th Group would be attached to the 7th Division."

"Which means?"

"Which means that the 4th Group's going to move, that's all."

"Where to?"

"Into billets at Azannes, I expect."

Feeling a little downcast at not having done anything,

we went back along the same road by which we had come, into the setting sun, now red in a halo of dust.

The glandered horse had lain down in the ditch. It was still breathing, and tossing its head from side to side to shake off the wasps that clung in yellow patches round its eyes and in its nostrils.

At Azannes, where we have come into billets, the horses are picketed in a plum-orchard, and, being worn out with the long march, the dust and the heat, leave me free to dream during my four hours on guard.

It is a marvellous mid-August night, infinitely starry and enlivened by falling stars that leave a long, phosphorescent trail; while searchlights from Verdun cast shifting bars of gold across the firmament.

The moon has risen, but scarcely penetrates the thick foliage of the plum trees, and the still camp is all in darkness. Only here and there it makes yellow patches on the grass or on the backs of the horses, which sleep standing. The comrade who is sharing the night-guard with me is lying under his greatcoat at the foot of a tall pear tree. Before me, as I write, the moon lights up the level plain. A veil of white gauze is spread over the fields. The two armies, with all fires extinguished, are asleep or watching.

SATURDAY, *August 15th.*

I was helping Hutin to clean the gun.

"Well, Hutin, war's a fine game, eh?"

"If it only means fooling about like this till September 22nd, when my time's up, I like it better than barracks. We've never been fed so well before. Let's hope it'll go on like this!"

"Let's hope it will. There are Boches about, though, unfortunately."

Reconnaissance.

(French dragoons in Belgium, August 1914.)

"Yes, that's the trouble."

"And then, too, we don't often get letters."

"That's a fact! Or rather we don't get them at all," said Hutin bitterly, thrusting the ramrod viciously down the barrel. "And as for the ones you send off," he added, "you're not allowed to say where you are, or what you're doing, or even to put the date on. I only wish I knew what you *are* allowed to say."

"All I put in mine is that it's fine weather and I'm still alive."

Still the same silence all along the line. It has lasted for four days now. What does it mean? For us who are merely pawns on the great chess-board the suspense is becoming dreadful. It affects one's nerves with the same tension that one sometimes feels when the sky is overcast with dark clouds, the moment before a storm bursts.

Saw General Boëlle. His car drew up on the road close to our park. He is a man with fine features, a cheerful expression, and a youthful face despite his white hair and moustache.

The old love of trophies has not diminished. Quite a crowd collected round a cyclist who came along from Mangiennes with a Mauser and two German packs made of cowhide.

It is remarkable how quickly instinct asserts itself on active service. Almost at once civilised man sinks into the background. Relationships become cruder. The need of making oneself respected usurps the first place in one's thoughts. One may not quite frankly confess this need, even to oneself, but one acts as if it were so.

Another thing is, that the weight of authority undergoes a change. That which an officer derives simply from his rank diminishes, while that which he owes to his character grows proportionately. Authority can only be measured in one way, and that is, by the confidence of the men in the worth of their commanders. Thus our own officer, Captain Bernard de Brisoult, in whom even the most hardened of us has recognised, beneath great charm of manner and kindness, a rare strength and intelligence, exercises an unbounded influence over us all, thanks to the confidence we feel in him. Yet he never in the least degree forces his personality as our commander on us. Captain de Brisoult never orders; he gives his commands in an ordinary conversational tone. But being an officer of innate distinction and tact, though he lives on intimate terms with the men, he always remains the captain. It would be hard to say whether he is more loved than respected or more respected than loved. And soldiers are good judges of men.

In the crude and masculine relationships between the men themselves there is ample room for real friendship; but it becomes rarer. The bonds of simple comradeship which subsisted in barrack life either disappear or are strengthened until they become definite though unexpressed pacts of devotion. The motive at the back of such pacts is rather egoism than the need for affection. You feel the necessity of having at your side a man on whose help you can at all times count, and whom you are equally resolved to help in any eventuality. In the bonds which are thus very firmly, though with no word said, established, deliberate selection necessarily operates. Affinity of character is not enough in itself. You assess, in the man who is to be your friend, his value as an aid in extremity, his courage, and also his physical strength.

SUNDAY, *August 16th.*

A heroic episode in our expedition of last Friday has only just come to my knowledge. It might be entitled, "The attack on the regimental train."

During our advance towards the enemy through the forest we were followed at a distance by our transport. When we turned back we passed them on the road, and they wheeled about and took their place in rear of the batteries. By the time the head of the column had almost reached Azannes, the tail was still in the middle of the woods. Dusk had set in. Suddenly, in the depths of the forest, a brisk fusillade broke out to right and left of the transport-waggons, while at the same time a loud noise of galloping came from behind. The sergeant who brought up the rear, and who was riding behind the forage-waggon—side by side with the cow that supplies the brigade with milk, which one of the men had charge of on the end of a long rope—convinced that the enemy had ambushed the column from the flanks and that it was about to be charged by a force of cavalry, immediately shouted, "Sauve qui peut! Uhlans!" at the top of his voice. The men jumped down off the waggons with their loaded rifles, and had no sooner done so when the column suddenly without any orders set off at a gallop. The men followed as best they could. But the horses of the forage-waggon, infuriated by the whipping they got, reared up and kicked over the traces and knocked over the cow, which began a struggle with its leader, and pulled wildly this way and that until in the end it shook itself free and went careering off into the cloud of dust left by the rapidly disappearing column.

A few seconds later the expected cavalry came along. The general commanding the artillery, with his staff and escort of chasseurs, had put our regimental train to flight. The fusillade came from two companies of the

103rd of the Line, who were concealed in the wood and had opened fire on a German aeroplane.

The weather has broken. Already yesterday evening a thunderstorm away to our left had startled us into thinking a cannonade had begun. And at stand-to this morning a heavy shower took us by surprise, so that we had to leave the coffee-pots on the fire while we sought refuge under the limbers or in the shelter of trees. Now it is raining slowly but steadily. If it goes on like this we shall have trouble with dysentery.

As we sat on ground-sheets drinking our coffee round the fire, while the battery cook stood over it like a guardian angel, my comrades asked me to read them a few pages out of my notebook. They wished me a safe home-coming in order that these notes of mine, which are so largely theirs too, may see the light.

"Shall you leave the names in?"

"Yes, unless you'd prefer me not to."

"No, leave them as they are. Then later on, if we come through, our old people and youngsters can read about us."

"If I'm killed, will you take charge of my notebook? I keep it here, in this pocket in my shirt."

Hutin reflected:

"Yes, only you know it's forbidden to meddle with the effects of the dead. You'd better put something in the book to show that that's what you want us to do."

He was right; and accordingly I wrote on the first page: "In case I should be killed, I ask my comrades to take charge of these papers until they are able to deliver them safely into the hands of my family."

"There, now you have duly made your dispositions

mortis causa," said Le Bidois, who was looking over my shoulder. And he added:

"It doesn't increase the risks."

Le Bidois is a long, thin fellow with a distinct look of the King of Spain, for which reason Déprez and I have christened him Alphonso. We greet him in the morning with a Montmartrois couplet:

> "*Alphonso, Alphonso,*
> *Veux tu te t'nir comme il fô !*"

We also call him "the Spanish grandee." He never takes offence.

"A corporal of pure gold," as his layer, Moratin, declares.

Teams of the 26th Artillery have brought back two of the limbers abandoned by the enemy at Mangiennes. They are painted a dull grey, and reminded me of the old 1890 material we used to drill with in the polygon at Le Mans.

They were followed by a pair of lumbering farm-waggons, great, long, narrow vehicles, full of packs, water-bottles, képis marked 130, mess-tins already blackened with the smoke of bivouac fires, brass-buckled belts, greatcoats with dark stains on them, and bayonets and rifles, red with rust and blood; a long blue flannel sash, dirty and sodden, was trailing in the mud behind one of the carts. These things had all been salvaged from the bodies of the unfortunate infantrymen killed at Mangiennes.

It was a melancholy sight in the steady downpour of rain, and moved us far more profoundly than all the descriptions we had had of Monday's fight.

Not long before, when taking the horses to water, I had seen, at the gate of the fortified cemetery at Azannes, a number of infantrymen lying asleep on the ground, sprawling anyhow, with their coats and equipment unfastened. They might have been dead. I imagined the bodies lying just so after Mangiennes. And the sight of their effects conjured up a further vision of the digging of trenches and the burying of those bodies. . . .

In the extraordinary quietness which has prevailed all along the line for a week, we had almost forgotten the work of death for which we are here.

At dusk, having swallowed our hot soup, we returned to our billet in a spacious barn full of comfortable straw. The village was thronged with troops of all arms. The blue dolmans of the chasseurs and the red trousers of the infantry made them conspicuous among the darker uniforms of artillery and engineers. One had to elbow one's way. A party of men carrying canvas buckets full of water in each hand shouted and swore for way to be made for them.

It was still raining. Thick blue smoke rose from the dunghills in front of the houses on either side of the road. The cavalrymen wore horse-cloths over their heads and shoulders, and many of the infantrymen were likewise hooded and cloaked in sacks and canvas sheets which they had found in the barns and farm-waggons. The crowd was for the most part silent; all were covered with mud and actuated by a single motive—to gain the shelter of their billets as quickly as possible. The only sound was of innumerable feet tramping in the mud. Four sappers, climbing up a ladder to the yawning window of a hay-loft, gave the impression of a monstrous cluster of dark grapes hanging in the air.

MONDAY, *August 17th.*

It was still raining when, in the early morning, we limbered up and marched off, preceded by the carts of salvaged equipment, looking still more lamentable and heart-rending.

We heard how a chasseur, a man whom I saw only yesterday (he rode a small bay mare), had been captured by the uhlans, who proceeded to tie him up, and then stuck a lance into his neck and bled him to death like a pig. This foul atrocity had actually been witnessed from behind a hedge by the peasant who told us of it, and who was still haggard with the horror of his experience.

Our horses had spent the night in the filth and mud. Their bellies, flanks and quarters were thickly plastered with manure, like ill-kept cattle, and their tails and manes were stiff with clayey mud. We ourselves, with lumps of earth and grass sticking to our heels, and muddied up to the knees, presented a more massive appearance even than usual in our dark, sodden cloaks which hung in stiff, heavy folds from our shoulders.

Moirey was our next billet, only some three miles from Azannes; but the road was blocked with troops and transport, and we had to halt and pull in to the side at frequent intervals.

The captain was continually giving the order:

"Dismount! Gunners off the limbers!"

Most of the men were tortured with diarrhœa, and profited by every opportunity to scatter over the fields.

At Moirey we found ourselves no better off than we had been at Azannes. An orchard was again allotted to us, and the grass immediately turned to mud under the horses' hoofs.

Our first task was to shovel earth over the excretions

left behind by other troops. The question of latrines is always a serious one. Little trenches are dug for the purpose near each camping-ground. But many of the men stubbornly refuse to make use of them. They prefer to squat down here or there, at the risk of being chased away with whips by those who object to their filth. A regular police patrol has to be maintained round the guns and horses. The severe punishments which our officers threaten to inflict on any man caught in the act outside the latrines are practically useless. It still goes on. And the major can only repeat:

"The filthy brutes!"

This evening gun-fire began quite close by.

Perhaps we are going to fight at last.

There was hardly any wood to be found. What we did manage to collect was damp, and sent up great clouds of acrid smoke which the wind beat down on us. The water for the soup had to be fetched from more than three hundred yards away, and had also to be shared with the horses. The ration bread was mouldy, and only just eatable after being toasted.

At watering-time the single village street was packed with horses either being led or ridden bare-back. Six batteries are billeted at Moirey, and there is only one water-trough, fed by a little dribble of spring-water not more than two fingers thick. Every twenty paces one had to halt, and it was all one could do to avoid being kicked. The men, exasperated by the slowness, shouted and swore at the least provocation.

At the end of five minutes one moved another twenty paces. And when at last we reached the trough, round which one waded ankle-deep in mud, the hundreds of horses before us had left so much slobber on the water that our own animals refused to drink.

The rumour goes that a great battle has been fought near Nancy, and that we are the victors. Why are not we too advancing?

TUESDAY, *August 18th.*

Lucas, the battery cyclist, succeeded in unearthing two bottles of champagne this afternoon. He secretly deposited them in the guardhouse, where Le Bidois, being corporal of the guard, watched over them.

Lucas is a young draughtsman of considerable talent. His character is written in his fresh, mobile, rather feminine face. When you meet him in the morning he takes you by the arm.

"Ah! old man . . . such a lark! The most ravishing little girl . . . a perfect darling. . . ."

And the same evening he will be saying:

"Ah! old man, I'm miserable! . . . Don't speak to me! I'm absolutely miserable! . . ."

In a neighbouring village, Damvillers, I believe, he has made the conquest of a fair tobacconist. Consequently he found pipes, notepaper, liqueurs and even champagne where no one else would have found anything at all.

At twilight he beckoned mysteriously to Déprez and me from the doorway of the guardhouse, where tall Le Bidois stood leaning on his sword. The guardhouse consists of a ramshackle hut which is only held together by the close embrace of an ivy plant. The door has but one hinge, and the wooden stairway to the loft has crumbled away into dust. In this charming retreat we peacefully drank the champagne out of our tin mugs.

WEDNESDAY, *August 19th.*

No. 1 gun possesses a combination which is the joy of the whole battery, namely, Astruc and his off-horse Jericho. Astruc, not much taller than a boot, with hardly any legs to him, a beak like a raven and a merry twinkle in his black eyes; and Jericho, an intractable brute that kicks, bites and refuses to be groomed. Astruc indulges in long conversations with him, and greets him every morning with the sort of affection one bestows on a rather whimsical old friend.

"Well, Jericho, what news? . . . Have you been dreaming of pretty Boche mares?"

Upon Bréjard's remarking that Jericho is a gelding:

"Oh well," says Astruc, "no doubt he often gets ideas in his head, all the same."

But to-day Jericho was in an ill humour. He objected to being bridled preparatory to being taken to water.

"Ah, I know what it is, old boy," said Astruc; "you haven't had your quid this morning. . . . It's your quid you want."

He held out a pinch of tobacco in the hollow of his hand, which the horse swallowed greedily. Then, when Astruc had mounted Hermine, his near-horse, Jericho snapped at the toe of his boot. And the more Astruc beat him, the more Jericho pulled.

"There's trouble in store for the Boches," said Astruc, "when I let Jericho loose among them; he'll lash out right and left and do them in by the dozen. If only there were a hundred more like him. . . ."

And he added, looking into Jericho's face:

"The funniest thing about the old ruffian is his eyes—they're just like a naughty girl's."

A pontoon detachment went by along the road, with the long canvas boats on waggons, keel upwards. Tied to the rear of the last waggon were a group of foundered horses that followed heavily with their heads hanging down, blear-eyed and piteous. Half an hour later, in the distance, where the road winds up and down over the hills, like a white ribbon in the sunlight, one saw the column nearing the top of a rise, as if about to ascend into the blue heavens. Men and horses were nothing but a dark, shifting line, but the canvas bottoms of the boats still gleamed. More troops are now going by along the road, column after column of them.

The health of the men is excellent, but the horses are adapting themselves with less success to this new manner of life. We had to abandon one on the road last Friday, and yesterday Defricheur, one of the old battery horses, died. A pit had to be dug to bury him in. Four men had been at work on the job for more than an hour, in hard stony ground, when the Mayor of Moirey arrived on the scene. The pit had been opened too close to the houses. The heavy carcase had to be dragged farther away and the work begun all over again. Unfortunately they miscalculated the measurements, and when the hole was dug to the proper depth Defricheur, an exceptionally large beast, would not go in. The men were tired of digging, so they broke the beast's legs with their picks and shovels and folded them in under its belly, by which means they were just able to force the carcase into the pit.

One can still see the fair hill which shut in our horizon when we were at Ville-devant-Chaumont; it stands out splendidly, as symmetrical as if a compass had traced it, and gleams like burnished bronze under the blue sky.

Moirey lies deep in the bosom of a valley. The houses are poor, with unevenly tiled roofs. In whatever direction you leave the village, a fold in the ground quickly masks it from view, so that you see nothing but the tops of the roofs and the squat, four-sided slate belfry, which hardly rises above them.

While we were grooming the horses by an iris-bordered stream in a meadow, a bevy of white sun-bonnets came fluttering down from the village. There was only a narrow foot-bridge over the stream; we barred the way with two horses, one at each end, and claimed a kiss by way of toll. The four young girls, with fresh, smiling faces beneath their great white butterflies of head-dresses, hesitated. One of them made a dash for it, jumped, and wetted herself, whereupon the others, profiting by this example, prepared to face the music.

"Come now, one kiss isn't dear in war-time," said Déprez.

They paid conscientiously.

FRIDAY, *August 21st.*

We awoke in thick mist, immediately limbered up, and were on the move before five o'clock. The surface of the road was badly cut up by the artillery which had been passing along it for three days on end, and we were jolted and shaken on the limbers till there was hardly a breath left in our bodies.

Fortunately the battery only advanced at a walk.

The mist had collected in the bottom of the valley up which the road wound. To the right, great rounded hilltops rose out of it, like islands. I was unable to withdraw my eyes from their symmetrical, divinely harmonious curves—the breasts of Cybele.

Then the road dawdled across a plain with broad undulations like the mighty heavings of an ocean swell. Innumerable sheaves of corn dotted the fields in all directions. There were few trees—only an occasional clump or short row of poplars. The mist massed them more solidly together and unified the shades of green.

There was no sound of battle.

We passed regimental trains and corps ambulances. The enemy was evidently nowhere in the vicinity.

Nevertheless, the country had been made ready for eventualities. A farm by the road had been put into a state of defence. The windows were barricaded with mattresses and bundles of straw; the garden wall was loopholed and crenellated; trenches had been dug across the fields as far as a wood, where an abattis had been constructed. Heaps of earth had been thrown up across the ditches on either side of the road, with ladders, two wheelbarrows, a plough, a roller, and bundles of straw piled in front of them. Two large carts barred the actual roadway, but had been pushed aside and lay up-ended, one on the right and one on the left, with their shafts pointing to the sky.

On and on we rolled across the melancholy, monotonous landscape. We hardly seemed to be advancing, so little did it vary.

The mists dispersed, and suddenly, without any previous indication of a change, as though by a miracle, an admirable view opened out before us. We found ourselves on a ridge between two valleys. On one side was a little narrow ravine, with a dark stream flowing through an emerald-green water-meadow along the foot of it, and thick woods covering its sides, wave upon wave, like enormous green cascades. The woods closed in on the meadow as though to set off and enhance its brilliance with their living fleece of deep, quivering, variegated green. In front of us rose a spur, with the rugged outline of a fortress, up which the road we were following wound in a succession of hair-pin curves. To the right, in contrast with the intimate, cool course of the little stream, a broad vale lay bathed in the sunshine, open, devoid of mystery, with yellowing crops lining its gradual, even curves. There was a river in the midst, barely discernible; but one could see roads, a railway line, villages, Vélosnes on one bank, on the other Torgny, their white walls and red roofs conspicuous among the fields.

Nothing in the scene suggested war. The far-away sound of gun-fire was no more alarming than a rumble of heavy wheels. It was a lovely day, made fairer still by the distance-softening haze. The narrow road we were following dipped down into the valley in a series of esses. The horses had a struggle to hold back the guns, and particularly the ammunition waggons, from running away with them down the slope. Their hoofs hesitated on the loose, rolling pebbles, and they advanced slowly and cautiously, arching their backs in the effort.

The river formed the Franco-Belgian frontier. A customs official was leaning with his back against the parapet of the bridge.

A voice cried:

"No fine linen or lace to-day, old man!"

Another asked:

"Any duty to pay on melinite?"

The man smiled.

This first Belgian village, Torgny, contrasted strongly with the French villages through which we had passed since the dawn. Ours had been dilapidated, dirty, noisome with the smell of dunghills, loudly eloquent of poverty. Torgny was gay and clean. There were curtains in the windows and here and there embroidered blinds. The shutters, doors and all the woodwork were painted a bright green.

The place seemed to welcome us with a placid, friendly smile. One had a glimpse through the windows of red-tiled floors; the copper of stoves and candlesticks shone in the dim light of the interiors and was reflected in the brightly polished furniture.

Our column halted in the middle of the village. The street was steep, and the wheels of our vehicles had to be securely wedged. A woman and a fair, slender, regular-featured little girl were sitting on the threshold of their house, which had a wistaria trained below the first-floor windows. We asked them where the road which our battery was following led to, and a conversation ensued. Both of them, mother and daughter—and also the grandmother, a little wrinkled old woman with brilliant eyes who came out to look at us—spoke with a drawling, sing-song accent that was by no means disagreeable.

"Have the Germans been as far as this?"

"Yes, monsieur. They came, but they did no harm . . . they hadn't time to. Five or six of them appeared in front of those woods up the hill there: mounted men. Then they went back. Some of the folks here saw them. There were some French cavalry soldiers here, men in blue and red uniforms."

"Chasseurs?"

"Likely enough. They were very nice, anyhow. As there were only a few of them at first, there were almost quarrels among us to have them in our houses. So then, when the uhlans came out of the woods, they saw the French and went back again."

"And have you had any Belgian soldiers here?"

"No, they've never been this way," said the grandmother, "but my granddaughter saw some last year at Arlon."

"Yes," the little girl added, "and their clothes are better than yours."

We made ourselves quite at home. They brought chairs out for us, and we sat and talked while waiting for the order to resume our march.

"You owe us a big candle," said the old grandmother. "We stopped them. They weren't expecting it. They thought they'd find sheep, and they found lions, yes, lions. They say so themselves."

We agreed with all our hearts. Truly we are assured for the future of the friendship of the Belgians. We are their ever grateful debtors. And there is no more solid affection than that which a benefactor feels for those whom he obliges. It is a feeling of superiority and pride, and a most pleasant feeling altogether.

Unquestionably the blood so valiantly shed for us in Belgium will be productive of more friendship between us than twenty years of effort to preserve the French language and culture from Germanisation. And forty years hence, when we meet a Belgian among us, he will say in his pleasing accent:

"Ah, well, you know, monsieur, without us, in 1914 . . ."

He will be glad to remind us of all that France owes to his glorious little country; better still, he will feel drawn towards us for that very reason.

"Make no mistake," the mother said to us, "it has cost us dear to defend our neutrality. It's frightful, the things the Germans have done! . . . The women are the ones they're most horrible to. There's one we know well, who lives in that part . . . they cut off her breasts . . . and then they ripped her open. And what they've done to so many others! It's dreadful, messieurs, dreadful! They must be worse than beasts! You must tell your people in France about these things, about all our country has been through. . . . Surely you won't be like that yourselves when you get into Germany?"

And the grandmother added:

"I'm an old woman, I'm seventy and more. I had never seen war in Belgium."

She spoke almost without anger, poor old creature, only with a great sadness in her tremulous old voice.

When orders came we found we were not to move any

farther, but to billet in Torgny for the night. As soon as the horses had been picketed and given their oats, Déprez and I hastened back to the house with the wistaria to see if we could purchase some milk and eggs. The grandmother was deeply grieved, but she had given all she had to the chasseurs. But she sent us a few doors farther down the street, to the house of one of her daughters who, she said, would milk her cow for us. She added, as we took our leave:

"We have a good barn with plenty of straw, where you would be quite warm and comfortable. So come back here for the night, messieurs."

When we came to the house which she had indicated we were welcomed as if we had been expected.

"Here are some gunners, maman," said a young woman with a child in her arms. "They've come for some milk."

The mother came out of an inner room.

"I'll milk the cow at once," she said. "Good morning, messieurs; won't you sit down? You must be tired."

Meanwhile Lucas had found some eggs.

"I expect you'd like an omelette," suggested the young woman; "it won't take a minute. But sit down, do sit down! Haven't you been standing long enough?"

In a few moments the fat was sizzling in the frying-pan.

Infantrymen and cavalrymen came continually to the door, and the two women distributed the milk from their cow, and were most unwilling to be paid for it. When there was no more left, they were deeply grieved at having to send away empty-handed the many men who still kept arriving.

"We've given all we have, mes pauvres messieurs," they said. "There's only just enough left over for the little girl. You see, we've only one cow."

A chasseur brought back a cooking-pot which they had lent him, and another borrowed a gridiron. Never were Frenchmen given such a reception in France.

Then our fair-haired little friend from up the street came in, with an earthenware milk-jug in her hand.

"Have you any milk, aunt? It's for some of the soldiers who are feeling ill. . . ."

"Ma pauvre petite fille, it's all gone except a few drops for baby."

"Oh, dear."

The girl saw us sitting at the table before the steaming omelette, and smiled to us as old acquaintances. I told her that, if and when I got home again, I intended to make a book of what I had seen at the war.

"And so, mademoiselle, will you tell me your name, so that I may send you my book as a souvenir, for you, your grandmother, your mother and your aunt, who have all been so kind to the French?"

"Monsieur, my name is Aline—Aline Badureau."

"Yours is a pretty name, Aline."

She stood in the doorway before going out.

"I wish you a safe return, monsieur," she said to me, "so that you may send me your book. But you'll forget, I know. They say no one forgets so quickly as a Frenchman."

I protested strenuously.

PART III

THE CLASH—THE RETREAT

SATURDAY, *August 22nd.*

WE slept in the old woman's barn, where the hay, as she had said, was deep and warm. At three in the morning a sentry roused us by shouting through the dormer-window, and we at once groped our way through the darkness to the horse-lines, and harnessed and hooked in.

After we had been moving for some time a thin, diffuse light began to spread over the face of the landscape. A mist, rising from the low fields, obscured the first glimmerings of the young day. So thick was the atmosphere that the next gun in front was hardly visible, and we who sat on the limber, facing to the rear, could only make out a moving shadow where the leading pair of the team behind was following at our heels.

In this manner we came to the little town of Virton. All the inhabitants were at their doors, and offered us coffee, milk, tobacco and cigars. The men jumped off the limbers and hastily swallowed the steaming liquid, while the drivers leant down over the necks of their horses and held out their mugs to be filled.

We asked for information:

"Have you seen the Germans?"

"Only two or three who came to buy socks and sugar. They won't be coming back now, eh?"

"What are *we* here for?"

The clear faces of the women, framed in corn-coloured hair, were absolutely calm. Chubby children, like

Rubens cherubs, ran along beside the column as it moved off, while others, a little older, shouted, "Vivent les Français!"

Our batteries took their place in rear of a group of the 26th Artillery on the Ethe road, a fine, straight highway with a line of tall trees on either side of it. The corn-sheaves in the fields looked so like the silhouettes of men that for a moment one was deceived into thinking there were some infantry there.

A field hospital had been installed in one of the villages through which we passed; mules bearing medical stores were drawn up in a sunken road.

We had scarcely left the last houses of this village behind us when a sudden fusillade broke out, like the crackle of a dry wood-fire. A machine-gun joined in, with a jerky rat-tat-tat like a cinematograph.

Fighting was going on somewhere quite close, to our front and right, in the fog. I listened. . . . I was all ears for the sound of bullets in the air.

"Right wheel!"

"Trot!"

What now? What was happening? What had become of the three batteries in front of us? We went along a road to the right. The firing ceased. This advancing through the fog, which seemed to grow denser and denser as we went, was nervous work. We were certain, this time, of the enemy's nearness.

At last the order was given to halt, it being then about seven o'clock. There was no more sound of fighting. We unbridled the horses to give them a feed, and then sat and lay in the grass by the side of the road, still half asleep.

The firing broke out again, but to our left now. How could our position have altered so with regard to that of the enemy? Only a few minutes before the fighting had been to our right. . . . But perhaps it had merely been a patrol that had lost its way. I gave up trying to understand; I had lost all sense of direction in the fog.

The noise was farther off this time. It began with a single, isolated shot, like a signal. Indeed, for a brief moment I thought it was the crack of one of our own drivers' whips. Then the rattle of musketry became general, reaching us in regular waves as though borne by a gusty wind, though actually there was not a breath stirring; the fog hung thick and motionless.

Then quite suddenly the sun appeared, and the mists vanished as if by magic. The effect was as of vast gauze curtains being raised towards the vault of heaven. In a few minutes the countryside was revealed throughout its extent. And immediately guns began firing.

To our right were some broad meadows, with cattle grazing, and farther off, hills and woods, and a village on a distant slope near the edge of a forest. To the left, northwards, the horizon was shut in by a semicircle of hills, quite close to us. In between flowed a river, draining the stubble-covered slopes, against which a large, bowl-shaped willow tree made a single blob of green.

Away up on the hill, where the corn was still standing, a battery was in position; one could see the four dark points of the muzzles of its guns.

Extending along the perfectly straight road, down the well-defined perspective of the avenue of tall trees, the twelve batteries of my regiment, with their waggons in rear of them, formed an interminable, motionless line.

The captain's voice broke the silence:

"Prepare for action!"

The men jumped up from where they had been lying on the grass, removed the leather breech and muzzle covers, fixed the sights and tested the traversing and elevating gears.

While we were so engaged a sudden explosion startled us. A little floating white cloud appeared above the battery over in the cornfield. It spread, then disappeared. And suddenly, in quick succession, six more shrapnel shells burst over the bowl-shaped willow tree.

I felt a growing uneasiness, as though the circulation of my blood was slowing down. I was not afraid. Indeed, there was no danger immediately threatening us, but I had an instinctive feeling that a great battle had begun and that we must be prepared to make a mighty effort to-day.

Nervousness made all our faces grave, and riveted our eyes to the point on the skyline where shells were now bursting continuously. We might not have confessed to this nervousness, but there was no more talking; we stood and waited for we scarcely knew what—the burst of a shell, the arrival of orders, anything.

In my heart I was not ashamed of being nervous; a baptism of fire must always be disturbing. And there we stayed, drawn up in column on the road; the enemy needed only to lengthen his range to be right on to us, entirely defenceless as we were.

These emotions, be it added, were only superficial. If there was a certain anxiety in our eyes, we were also smiling, and fully determined to do all that should be required of us to turn the coming battle into a French victory.

The colonel commanding the regiment rode by, accompanied by Captain Maunoury and a staff of lieutenants. He surveyed us with a calm, penetrating look that both appraised and encouraged us. The little troop of horsemen rapidly receded into the distance, up the slope which the enemy was bombarding.

"Stand by!"

We were going into action. . . .

On the side of the semicircle of hills some sections of infantry were advancing by short rushes in extended order. The men suddenly got up, ran forward, and as suddenly, at an inaudible word of command, threw themselves down and disappeared as if into a trap. They moved in this fashion farther and farther away, until at last one saw them for an instant darkly silhouetted against the sky as they went over the ridge.

The heat became intense, it being now about ten o'clock. From the unknown country beyond the hills came the terrific noise of the battle: the rattle of musketry and the roar of machine-guns, like great rollers being sucked back on a pebbly shore, and the thunder of artillery enveloping and uniting all these noises into a single voice like that of a storm in mid-ocean, with heaving, crashing waves, deep, thudding undertones and the shrill whistle of the wind through the surf.

The line of battle appeared to run east and west, with the Germans holding the north and the French the south.

"En avant!"

A stream, half hidden in the long grass, ran through the fields which we had first to cross. The men jumped down off the limbers and led the off-horses by the bridle. The drivers spurred the team to a trot. The soft soil yielded under the wheels, and despite the efforts of the horses the heavy waggon sank up to the axles in the mud. With a mighty heave it was dragged free.

God, where were we going? Where were we going? . . . Towards the bowl-shaped willow tree, towards those heights where for two hours now the hail of German shrapnel had been pouring down continuously, not sparing an acre. Why were we being led there, of all places? Weren't there plenty of other good positions on those hills? We should be massacred! . . . The column moved steadily forward, at a walk, towards the sloping field where shell after shell was bursting every minute.

Why? Why? Death had been falling there without pause since the fog lifted. And we were going straight towards it.

I was half choking with nervousness, but my brain was under control. I perfectly understood that the time had come for me to sacrifice my life. We were going to that hill, all of us were going there, and not all of us would come back. Simple!

The seething blend of animality and thought which was my life would soon be still. My bleeding body would be stretched on the ground. I could see it. Suddenly, I thought, over the far perspective of the future, which is always flooded with sunshine, a great curtain drops. It's finished! It won't have been very long; I'm only twenty-one.

I neither argued nor hesitated. If it was my destiny to be sacrificed that higher destinies might be fulfilled, very well. My fate was the fate of my country, of all that I loved, of all that at that instant I most yearned for. If I must die, die I must. That's over, I thought; and was surprised that it was not more difficult.

We still advanced at a walk, with the drivers on foot at their horses' heads. We reached the bowl-shaped tree. Suddenly we heard, swiftly approaching from far away, a faint noise of wings, an unfolding of some silky material. It grew and swelled into a buzzing of hornets. The shell was coming straight at us—and then something indescribable—the very air became sonorous, became one great throb, and the throbbing was communicated to our flesh, our nerves, the very marrow in our bones. The men crouched against the limber-wheels, the drivers cowered behind their horses, waiting for the crash. . . . A second, two seconds, three seconds . . . hours. I shrank and hunched up my shoulders; I was shivering. I felt the instinct to run away; it ran through all my body: I was the beast terrified of death. . . . Crash! ! ! The thunderbolt seemed to have fallen at my feet. The shrapnel bullets whizzed through the air in a great blast of wind.

And then on that very spot, in that potato-field that was so torn with shrapnel and high explosive that it was difficult to find a way for the guns between the shell-holes, the column halted.

What were we waiting for? At least let us get into position. . . . Let us answer the enemy, shoot back at him! . . . It seemed to me that if we could only hear the bark of our seventy-fives the anguish of these mortal moments would be less acute. . . . We needed to fight, not simply to stand there and be blown to bits. . . . And there we stayed, perfectly still.

More shells, which seemed to graze us almost, shook me from head to foot and made the gun shield behind which I was crouching vibrate. Fortunately the ground sloped steeply, and they fell behind us. I sweated . . . I sweated with fear . . . though I knew that I shouldn't run, that I should let myself be killed in my place. . . . But why couldn't we do something?

Then an order came at last and we set off again. The drivers could hardly control their teams; the horses were maddened and pulled in all directions.

Hutin, jerking his chin up, said:

"You're absolutely green, old man!"

"So are you, if you could only see yourself!" I answered.

A shell burst just in front of the team, throwing up a fountain of earth and wounding the middle driver. The man rolled over on the ground.

"Forward!"

A little short of the crest we moved into position, on the edge of a field of oats. The waggons withdrew into cover somewhere towards Latour, whose church-tower we could see sticking up in a valley to our left. Crouching behind the shields of the gun, we waited for the command to open fire. But the captain, from where he knelt in the corn in front of the battery, could make nothing out. We gathered from him that a thick mist was still floating over the woods near Ethe and Etalle where the enemy were. All round us, meanwhile, overhead and behind the guns, high explosive and shrapnel of all calibres burst without respite, plastering the position with bullets and splinters. It seemed impossible for us to escape death. . . . Behind our gun there was a little ditch. I lay flat in it, waiting for the order to begin shooting. A big bay riding horse, with a red stream pouring from a gaping wound in its chest, stood motionless in the middle of the field.

The whistling of bullets, the crash of bursting shells, the reports of enemy batteries and of a neighbouring battery of seventy-fives, made it impossible to distinguish one sound from another in the echoing inferno of iron, flames and smoke. I was sweating still. My body quivered rather than trembled. The blood boiled in my head, beat against my temples: an iron belt gripped my belly. Unconsciously, like a lunatic, I found myself humming a chorus that we had been singing lately in billets, and which haunted me:

"*Trou là là, ça ne va guère,*
Trou là là, ça ne va pas !"

I was thinking all the time: "I shall die in this *trou* (hole)." Something grazed my backside. . . . "I'm hit!" . . . No, a shrapnel bullet had merely torn the seat of my breeches.

A cloud of black, evil-smelling smoke enveloped the battery. Someone was groaning. I raised my head to look, and through a sort of dirty fog saw Sergeant Thierry lying at the edge of the corn, with the six men of his gun gathered round him in a ring. The shell had burst right under his gun, smashing the buffer and putting the piece out of action.

Kneeling side by side, Captain de Brisoult and Lieutenant Hély d'Oissel were searching the horizon through their field-glasses. I admired them with all my heart. The sight of my two officers, and of the major calmly walking to and fro behind the battery with his arms folded, made me ashamed of my trembling. A furious, confused struggle took place within me. At the end of it I felt I had waked out of a sort of feverish torpor, full of hideous nightmares. I was no longer afraid. When I lay down again in my ditch, having nothing else to do, since we were not firing, instinct had yielded, and I had quite stopped trembling.

Then I became aware of a horrible smell in the ditch.

"Phew, there's a stink here!" I grunted.

Astruc was lying flat in the very bottom of it, a yard or two away from me. In a voice that seemed to rise from the depths of the earth, he answered:

"Don't you worry about that, old man! I'm lying in a t-rd if you want to know, and I wouldn't move for twenty francs!"

A line of infantrymen now appeared over the ridge, retiring. The noise of machine-guns was getting closer. It was quite clearly audible through the din of the bombardment.

The enemy must be advancing and our troops giving way. . . .

The German batteries which had been firing at us lengthened their range. Whole companies of infantry began retiring over the ridge.

Our officers conferred together.

"Can't do anything without orders. And there are no orders," the major repeated.

And we waited on. The tall lieutenant had got his revolver out. The men loaded their rifles. The German artillery, perhaps for fear of hitting their own advancing infantry, stopped firing. At any moment the enemy might appear over the ridge.

"Order up the limbers "

The manœuvre was soon completed.

Thierry, badly wounded in the knee, had of course to be brought away. He was in great pain, and didn't want to be touched. In spite of his protests three men lifted him up and laid him along the observation-ladder. He was very pale and seemed on the point of fainting. He murmured:

"Oh, you're hurting me! Let me be!"

The other wounded, five or six in number, hoisted themselves on to the limbers, and the battery set off at a brisk trot towards the Latour road.

The battle was lost. I knew neither why nor how. I had seen nothing. The French right must have given way considerably, for I now noticed shells bursting over some woods a long way off to the south-west, which had been nowhere near the fighting-line in the morning. It looked as though our flank must have been completely turned. A horrible thought assailed me. Was our line of retreat still clear? We crossed the railway line, fields, a stream, and reached the range of wooded hills that ran parallel with those which the army had occupied in the morning. On them, no doubt, we should be able to take up a new position. The drivers urged on their horses, while the rest of us jumped down off the limbers to lighten the load and ran along in extended order on either flank of the column. The narrow road was badly cut up and its surface strewn with loose pebbles. Half-way up the steep hillside a broken-down infantry waggon was straddled right across the way, completely barring it. A wretched white horse was straining in the shafts while the driver shouted and pushed at one of the wheels; but the waggon stuck fast.

One of our corporals hailed the infantryman:

"Get on, you there!"

Get on! get on! As if he could! Without letting go of the wheel for fear it might run back on him, he turned a pitiful face to us, and I could see the tears in his eyes.

"Get on? . . . Tell me how, I'd like to know!"

We went to his assistance, and by our united efforts the waggon was soon pushed over on to the grass to make room for our passage.

It was nearly two o'clock. The air was hot and oppressive. Apparently the battle was over: the only sound of firing came now from far away to the left, towards Virton and Saint-Mard.

Our column extended in a dark line up the side of the hill. We went on through the woods that crowned the heights, in quest of a way on to the plateau farther back. The horizon broadened. Suddenly, from the direction of Latour, a machine-gun opened fire. I motioned with my hand as if to drive away a wasp buzzing in my ear.

"It's us they're shooting at!" shouted Hutin.

Bullets hissed by us. They were firing from the hill we had left half an hour before. One of the horses was hit and sank to its knees. It was at once unharnessed and let loose. A man was hit through the thigh a moment later, but staggered on.

Then we came to a dip in the ground, enough to give cover from the machine-gun, where a field drove a wedge of green grass into the forest. Here our batteries drew up to await orders. I at once recognised how critical our position had become. There was no road through the woods on to the plateau. Several teams of the 10th Battery were held up on a forest track and could neither go forward nor come back. One gun was embedded up to the axles. To get away from our present situation we should have to go either right or left across the level fields, under direct fire from the machine-guns, and very likely also of whatever artillery the enemy had been able to bring up. The longer we waited, the less chance should we have of getting clear.

Then, too, how long would our line of retreat across the plateau remain open? We were clearly outflanked, with the enemy advancing on us from the semicircle of hills. The village of Latour was probably in his hands by now.

The major was waiting for orders. He spoke shortly, with abrupt gestures. His jaws came together with a snap, a sign of nervousness with which we were familiar; "he's cracking nuts," the men said. He had sent off a corporal in search of instructions; but where was the man to look for the staff at such an hour, with the army in full retreat?

A dragoon galloped up and dismounted before our officers. We gathered anxiously round. He brought information: the retirement was being carried out towards the right, along the Ruettes road. The enemy was through Latour and advancing on Ville-Houdlemont.

Our column at once moved off. Lieutenant Hély d'Oissel rode on ahead to pick out our route. The machine-gun opened fire again from the distance, but this time we heard no whistle of bullets. A fence held us up for a moment until we broke it down with our axes. The open ground we had to cross was of no great extent, consisting only of a single whale-backed field. Once across that we came to a sunken road, and so reached Ruettes.

A general was there, by the church, with no staff and an escort of only three dragoons.

The main road from Ruettes to Trellancourt was like a river in flood.

A passage had to be driven by main force through the retreating waves. Abreast of our column of artillery marched such infantry battalions as still had officers to command them. And to right and left, tossed hither and thither like bits of cork, now diverted into eddies, now pushed into the ditch, now carried along by the torrent, broken remnants of troops encumbered the way: wounded men, limping men, exhausted men, men without rifles or equipment, men who had lost touch with their units—all moving listlessly and slowly. Some of them tried to catch hold of our vehicles as we went past; one or two actually managed to hoist themselves up on to the limbers, while others allowed themselves to be dragged along like lay-figures.

While the retreating infantry continued along the main road, our own column turned off to the right up a steep lane leading on to the plateau. The day was drawing to a close. The dark mass of the Guéville woods, between ourselves and the sun, cast its shadow as far as the side of the next hill. The only troops here besides ourselves were stragglers. But there were many wounded men in the ditches on both sides of the road. They had halted for a short breathing-space before continuing the ascent. Not all of them would move on. As they lay there in the grass one saw more than one mask that already reflected the hollow face of death. Bright, feverish, wide-open eyes blinked slowly and heavily, staring blankly out at nothing from sunken sockets; hair was plastered across foreheads with sweat that ran in streaks down faces with puffed-out cheeks and pinched noses, grimy with dust and powder. Hardly any of these wounded men were bandaged. The blood had formed great dark patches on their coats, and splashed and streamed over the cloth. There was no sound of groaning or moaning. Two men without arms or equipment were urging on a little infantryman whose shoulder had been laid open by a piece of shell. Very pale, with his eyes shut, and with a stubborn, weary movement of his head, he was refusing to let them carry him. Several men with leg-wounds were limping along, using their rifles as crutches.

"Give us a lift!" they implored us.

We made room for them on the limbers. At each jolt of the road a fat bugler, with a bullet wound in his chest, uttered a long-drawn sigh of pain.

In the grass on both sides of the road lay packs that had been thrown away and had burst open, disgorging shirts, drawers, brushes, a forage-cap. All down the middle of the road were boots, mess-tins, cooking-pots flattened by wheels and horses' hoofs, underclothing, bayonets, ammunition pouches, loose cartridges gleaming in the dust, képis, broken rifles. The sight of these things was heart-rending. It was impossible not to think of the roads of defeat in August 1870, after Wissembourg and Forbach. And yet for a month past all the talk had been of victories: we had pictured Alsace won back, Germany open for our advance. And at the first clash here was the army, our army, beaten! With a sort of amazement I told myself that I had witnessed and taken part in a defeat.

We came to the end of the Guéville woods, which were being held by some soldiers of the 102nd Infantry Regiment. The road was still strewn with arms and equipment. The surface had been badly cut up by the passage of artillery and transport, and the wounded on our jolting limbers had the faces of men crucified.

I asked the fat bugler:

"How about stopping and putting you down if this shakes you too much?"

"No, I don't want the brutes to catch me."

"All the same, you're——"

"No, it's all right, it's all right."

And he bit his lip to prevent himself crying out. I was very tired. My skull was heavy and echoing with noise. Ah, for a sleep, a sleep, no matter where!

A short distance beyond the woods the battery turned aside into a field of cut corn, near a village called La Malmaison, and halted. I flopped down on some straw. If we were going to stop here we should have no chance of sleep; the enemy was too near. We should certainly be attacked during the night. And all I could think of was sleep. My one wish was that we should get far enough back to be able to sleep. I waited for the fatal word, "Unhook!" that would mean our staying in this field to fight within an hour, or perhaps sooner. But new orders came; we filed into the road again and went on, through La Malmaison, which was thronged with troops in disorder. Night was coming on. I felt I had reached the uttermost limit of exhaustion. I began to be oblivious of my surroundings. I saw, as if in a dream, the men hunched up on the limbers with lolling heads, the drivers swaying in their saddles as if they were drunk. I could vaguely hear a man of the 26th Artillery, who was on my own limber, telling how the three batteries which had preceded us in the morning along the Ethe road had been caught in column by the enemy machine-guns and captured entire, and how he himself had succeeded in escaping, almost alone, under cover of the fog.

In the darkness the noise of our jolting, clattering vehicles was like a bombardment in our ears. A long pole dragging in the road sounded to me exactly like a machine-gun. What an obsession! The column rolled on and on through the darkness, its endless, monotonous rumble unbroken by any voice or word of command.

At the end of a very long march we found ourselves, at about midnight, at Torgny again, where we billeted. No attempt was made to call the roll. Once through the door of the barn, I fell on my face in the straw, and it seemed to me, when I felt sleep envelop me, as if I was dying.

SUNDAY, *August 23rd.*

We were left to sleep in peace till past eight o'clock. Immediately we were roused we took the horses to water in a large trough in the middle of the village. The church bells were ringing, and I realised with something of a shock that there were still Sundays. . . . I was only half awake; my limbs were numb and I felt dog-tired. It was a painful effort to climb into the saddle. What would I not have given for a day's rest!

Returning to billets boot to boot with Déprez, we passed Mademoiselle Aline, wearing her best shoes and a light dress with a pattern of pink flowers, on her way to Mass. She recognised us, and smiled and waved.

When we got back to the battery they were waiting for us.

"Harness and limber up!"

"What, more shooting this morning?"

"Presumably. . . . I don't know," answered Bréjard. "Limber up! Look sharp!"

The two batteries which now constituted the group, our own and the 12th—the 10th having apparently fallen into the hands of the enemy in the Guéville woods—moved off along the road from Virton. Everything pointed to immediate action.

But almost at once we were halted in double column in a cornfield at the side of the road, where a large force of artillery was already formed up. The field was on an upward slope, and the batteries and teams made dark rectangles against the golden stubble.

There we called the roll. There were several empty places. Bâton, our middle driver, had been left with the ambulance at Torgny with a wound in the head; Sergeant Hubert was missing; Driver Homo, missing. I had last seen Homo with drawn features staggering across the field through the thick of the enemy shelling.

Lucas, the captain's cyclist orderly, a jolly young fellow, always laughing, and a particular friend of mine, was also missing. It was his fate that chiefly worried me.

In addition, all our waggons, under Lieutenant Couturier, had disappeared into the blue.

The captain gathered us round him in a circle to reorganise. There were only three guns for us to deal with; the fourth, which had had its buffer smashed, had to be sent back for repair.

I was so tired that as soon as I stood still I found myself going to sleep.

Hutin opened a tin of bully for the pair of us.

"Hungry, Lintier?"

"Hardly at all . . . though I haven't eaten anything since the night before last."

"Same here. D'you think we're going into it again to-day?"

"I suppose so."

Hutin pondered a moment. Then:

"The one thing that absolutely amazes me," he said, "is that we're still here."

"Yes, it is amazing."

"It's curious we haven't heard any more firing yet to-day."

"They don't seem to have advanced as they might have after their victory yesterday."

"What I think," declared the layer, "is that we were ambushed. They were waiting for us. They had those hills taped beforehand, and let us just walk into it. But it'll be a different story next time!"

"I should hope it will. My God, I want to sleep. Don't you too?"

"I do that."

We both swallowed a few mouthfuls of bully, without any appetite. Hutin closed the tin up just as orders arrived for the battery to move.

We went across country to Lamorteau, a considerable town on the Chiers, where we parked pending further orders.

In a few seconds fires were lit along the river-bank, the smoke from which went straight up into the warm, still morning air. The gunners made soup while the drivers fetched water for the horses, which were kept in harness.

And, while we were so engaged, who should appear on the bridge over the Chiers but Lieutenant Couturier at the head of his column. Lucas was with him. He came straight to me.

"Lucas!"

"Yes, old man, here I am."

"You old devil, you did give us a fright!"

We shook hands warmly, and, though nothing more was said, I felt enormously relieved.

Hubert was there too. As we sat round the fires waiting for the soup to get hot we told our respective stories. Then, no orders arriving, we slept. In the evening we went back to Torgny.

The major ordered the horses to be unharnessed, so that evidently no immediate action was expected. I stretched and yawned with satisfaction. But to form our bivouac was a labour in itself. The guns had to be put at intervals of twenty yards, and ropes stretched from wheel to wheel across the intervening space for the horses, so that when the latter had been duly fastened along the ropes, and the harness piled on the limber-poles, the whole park formed an even quadrilateral.

We took our coats off to the work, for it was still hot. Déprez was making out the feeds, while the drivers held out the nosebags of their teams, when someone suddenly shouted:

"'Plane over!"

"It's a Boche!"

Looking up, we saw a great bird with a forked tail, a vicious-looking bird of prey, swooping down from the sky right over the park. The men ran for their rifles and opened fire, bending backwards in their shirt-sleeves, with bare chests, at the low-flying German hawk. The frightened horses neighed, reared and pulled at the picket-ropes; several of them got free and galloped about the centre of the park. The bird seemed to waver.

"He's hit."

"He's coming down!"

"No, it only looks like it as he gets farther off."

The men still went on firing, long after the aeroplane had passed out of range.

The single village street was soon thronged with men leading horses to water or riding them bare-backed, while the air reverberated with shouts to make room at the water-trough, cries of recognition, oaths from men on foot who were knocked into by men on horseback—all the noise and pother of an artillery cantonment. A chasseur appeared, shouting and swearing as he forced his way through the human torrent.

"Hey! You're in no more hurry than the rest!" cried a voice.

"Yes, I am, though. Get back to your billets at once. I've got orders."

"What's up?"

"All troops have got to clear out of here. . . . No time to waste, either; the Germans are quite close. There's a hot time coming!"

As he spurred his horse on we hurried back to the battery. Had we been taken by surprise? We harnessed and hooked in at top speed, and before we had time to button up our coats the first gun was in motion.

"Walk, march! . . . Trot!"

We had to throw the nosebags, still half full of oats, on to the limbers and guns, and fasten them up as we ran alongside. Then, still half undressed, we scrambled up into our seats with the battery already moving at full speed down the rough, uneven road.

We kept constantly looking to our rear, towards the

hills that dominated Torgny to the east, round which we expected to see the heads of the enemy's columns appear at any moment. My ears were on the alert for the rattle of a machine-gun or the scream of an approaching shell.

The road down in the valley was black with teams and guns retiring at a trot in thick clouds of dust. Other batteries were moving across the fields. What could be the meaning of this sudden withdrawal? There had been no sound of gun-fire all day, except far away to the north, and even that had ceased. What then? It looked as if we had been taken by surprise, or very nearly so. But all our actions were equally incomprehensible, and no one knew anything.

We took up a position on the high ground between the rivers Chiers and Othain, from which during our advance we had seen all the wide green landscape bathed in sunshine. The effect that had then been made on me by that serenely majestic view seemed now to be buried in the distant past. I seemed to have aged ten years in a single day. It was a strange and intimately painful sensation.

From this position the muzzles of the guns threatened Torgny and the hills above it. At any moment we might have to fire on the unhappy village, and a shell from our own gun might shatter the very house that had given us shelter, might kill the women whose kindness and hospitality had meant so much to us.

The thought was unbearably painful. Accursed war!

But night came on without the captain having detected any movement or sign of the enemy. Behind us the narrow valley of the Othain filled with shadows. The waggons were parked two hundred yards from the battery. It was forbidden to make fires or even to light a lantern. Our safety to-morrow depended upon our not being observed. There were stars visible, but their brightness was veiled by a thin mist. There was no moon. Motionless, in dark masses, the horses quietly munched the oats in their nosebags. A great red glow appeared in the east, doubtless from where Malmaison was in flames. And as the darkness increased, to the right and left of this great glare other glares showed. Villages were burning everywhere. The backs of the horses, their heads and twitching ears, and the heavy bulk of the limbers showed up darkly against a lurid sky.

Hutin and I stood together with folded arms, looking over the burning land.

"Oh, the savages . . . the savages!"

"So they call that war, eh?"

And we both fell silent, overcome with horror and rage. I saw a yellow gleam, reflected from the glowing sky, in my friend's dark eyes.

"And to think they're too strong for us . . . that we can't stop it! . . . My God!"

"It'll come. . . ."

"Yes, it'll come . . . and they shall pay for it."

We went and lay down in the straw spread behind our gun. A searchlight from Verdun regularly swept across the landscape. An optical telegraph threw luminous bars into the heavens. And we fell asleep, huddled one against another, with one man on sentry standing in his cloak by the gun.

MONDAY, *August 24th.*

It was still pitch-dark when a shadowy form shook me by the shoulder.

"Stand to!"

"What's the time?"

"Don't know," answered the sentry who had roused me.

Out in front the villages were still burning. Groping about in the darkness, and almost without a sound, we harnessed and hooked in. The waggons came up and took their place behind the guns. A steep descent. . . . Loose stones on the road. The horses stumbled and were in danger of falling at every step; the brakes had little effect, and we had to jump down and hang on behind, letting ourselves be dragged along, to prevent the limber from bearing down on the hindmost pair of the team.

At dawn we went through a dead village. Five chasseurs were asleep at the foot of the high church wall. They had their arms through the reins of their horses, which were standing motionless beside them, also asleep. A pale, cold light filtered through the thick mist which had collected at the bottom of the valley. The air was fresh and cold. We moved at a walk, in silence, the men dozing in their seats. We were going westwards. Retiring. Why? Hadn't we been well placed, up on the hill, to await the enemy? A silvery sun appeared through the mists, in a halo.

After a long halt in a lucerne field thickly spread with manure, the smell of which clung to us long afterwards, we took up a firing position on a hill near Flassigny. But almost immediately new orders came and we set off again, still westwards. We had a glimpse, through a gap between two hills, of a distant town—presumably Montmédy.

About the middle of the day we halted again on the road—in a valley, near a stream.

"Dismount! Loosen girths! Stand easy!"

The sun was burning hot, without a breath of wind in the air. We had nothing in our water-bottles but some tepid, brackish water from the Othain. That of the stream was undrinkable, and useless for anything except a wash. The men slept in the ditches at the side of the road, and the horses stood motionless, overcome with the heat.

It was dusk when our group received orders to proceed to Marville.

I recognised the town when we reached it. We had passed through Marville on our way up to Torgny. Then it had been a cheerful little place, with flower-gardens and summer-houses on the river-bank, and masses of dahlias. To-day Marville was deserted. Great farm-waggons crammed with bedding, chests of drawers and baskets, were standing in the street ready to move. In one cart I noticed a canary's cage next to a child's perambulator and a tiny cradle. And among all these things sat women, with their children round them. They were in tears; the children were huddled against their skirts. Dogs lay under the carts, waiting to follow them. We asked these poor people where they were going.

"We don't know. They say we must get away quickly. We're leaving now. . . . How we'll manage, with all our little ones, we don't know."

They questioned us:

"Tell us which direction it's safe to go in? We don't know anything. . . ."

Neither did we ourselves; however, we gave them the best indication we could:

"Over there. Go that way."

That way was westwards. Poor people!

We bivouacked just outside the town. A stream ran close by; in a stubble-field on the far side of it were two dead horses.

While we were settling in, the captain commanding the 10th Battery rode up on his horse. We had thought his battery was captured. But he told the major how, in the Guéville woods, he had succeeded in saving all four guns, though he had to abandon his waggons. His battery, he said, was in position on the high ground to the south-east of Marville. He had come for orders.

I was greatly inconvenienced by the rent made by a shrapnel bullet in the seat of my trousers the day before yesterday. Being divided between the wish to make a temporary repair and the fear lest a sudden order to move should surprise me with my trousers off, I let the whole of the peaceful evening go by without accomplishing this urgent job.

TUESDAY, *August 25th.*

The sun woke me. I shook myself.

"A pretty good night, eh, old Hutin?"

Hutin, who was still three parts asleep, made no reply. Déprez' voice called:

"Feeds!"

No one hurried. Two men still lay asleep, a dark heap of blue-black cloth in the straw under the limber. I heard a whistling noise that seemed familiar, and instinctively turned round to see what was causing it.

"Lie flat!" shouted a voice.

The men threw themselves down where they were. A shrapnel burst high up, right over the park. In the still air the thick smoke left by the explosion hung motionless among the trailing clouds of grey morning mist.

"We owe this to that aeroplane that came over yesterday," declared Hutin, whom the noise had fully roused.

"Yes, but they're shooting too high."

"That was only a ranging round. They'll be on to us properly in five minutes, you'll see."

"Now then, harness and limber up! Hurry!"

The park sprang to life. The men rushed to the horses

and vehicles, and in the twinkling of an eye the traces were hooked in and the teams ready to move off. Another shell came hissing through the air. We ducked without interrupting the work. By now high explosive shells were falling in Marville, and others hurtled screaming over our heads and burst along the neighbouring ridge, where the enemy doubtless supposed there were French guns in position. The drivers, crouching over the collars of their horses, plied their whips vigorously and the column set off at a trot. We took up a position on the high ground that overlooked the town, the Othain valley and the hills on the farther side of the river, from which direction the enemy was advancing. A hail of lead, steel and fire was pouring down on Marville. One of the first shells had hit the church tower. From our position the town itself was invisible, but great black columns of smoke were mounting straight up into the sky. Marville was in flames. In the din of the bombardment—which had swollen till it was a continuous thundering blast, increasing, diminishing, echoing round the hills, rolling, booming, crashing, never ceasing for a moment—it was difficult to distinguish between the noise of the German guns and our own artillery. But as one's ears grew accustomed to it, one recognised through the storm the staccato bark of the seventy-fives.

"Stand by! Layers to me!"

The layers ran to the captain.

"To our front, a fan-shaped tree. . . ."

"Aiming point, that tree. . . . Angle of sight, zero . . . All guns, 150 degrees right. . . ."

The layers ran back each to his respective gun and laid it. The breech closed over the inserted round. The layer raised his arm:

"Ready!"

"One round!" came the warning command.

The crew stood aside by the wheels of the gun, and

the firing-number bent down to catch hold of the lanyard.

"Fire!"

The gun springs back like a frightened beast. A tongue of flame leaps from the muzzle. Your skull vibrates, a thousand bells ring and peal in your ears, you shake from head to foot. The blast from the explosion has raised a cloud of dust. The ground trembles. You have a taste in your mouth that is insipid to begin with, then bitter: the taste—or it is almost more like a sensation —of powder. Rapid fire continues without pause. The men's movements are orderly, precise and quick. There are no words spoken: gestures suffice to indicate the familiar routine. All you hear is the elevation order, shouted by the captain and repeated by the No. 1 of each gun.

"Two thousand five hundred!"

"Fire!"

"Two thousand five hundred and twenty-five!"

"Fire!"

After the first round the gun is "settled." The layer and the firer are installed in their seats behind the shield. After each round the barrel recoils along the hydraulic buffer-guides, then evenly and exactly moves forward again "into position," ready for the next. Behind the gun a heap of smoking, empty shell-cases accumulates.

"Cease fire!"

The men lay down in the grass. Some took the opportunity to light a cigarette.

Another aeroplane: the same dark bird of prey outlined against the pale blue of the gradually lightening sky.

We were filled with rage. What a subjection! The man was calmly noting our position. A minute later the enemy opened fire with heavy artillery along the crest we occupied and on a neighbouring wood. It was time to change our position, for the most dangerous moment for us is when the teams come up for the guns. A battery is then extremely vulnerable.

Before the enemy had time to range we limbered up and moved away into a hollow depression in the plateau. Great level fields extended all around, bristly with stubble. There was no green in all the bare landscape except where a line of poplars bordered a road to our left. In front and to rear of us were empty trenches. Marville was still burning. The smoke had made a vast black smear across the eastern sky. The sun was now well up, and the glare on the stubble was dazzling. We were beginning to feel the effects of heat and thirst. The din of the battle grew louder and louder.

The captain noticed through his field-glasses, at the foot of some distant hills, still blue with mist, to the south-east, a column of artillery or a train of lorries and great masses of infantry on the march. Were they French troops? Or was it the enemy? He was unable to decide. The mist and the distance made it impossible to distinguish the uniforms.

"We can't fire on them," he said; "they may be French."

Standing up on a limber, with his glasses to his eyes, he stared and stared at this new danger.

"If it's the enemy, they're outflanking us. . . . outflanking us. They're just going into a wood . . . we shan't be able to see them any more. . . . Run and ask the commanding officer if he knows."

But the major was equally in the dark. His orders contained no reference to those hills. He, too, was peering across at them through his glasses, but could make nothing of the moving columns. And he, in turn, muttered, "If it's the enemy, they're outflanking us."

A mounted scout was sent off at the gallop. We waited in a state of nervous tension.

A solitary infantryman, without pack or rifle, had stopped near No. 4 gun.

"Are you hit?" he was asked.

"No."

"Where 're you from?"

The captain signalled for the man to be brought to him. But the man had thrown his arms away and was slow to obey.

"What troops are those over there?" the captain asked him. "Are they French?"

"I don't know."

"Well, where have you come from, anyway?"

The infantryman made a great sweep with his arm that covered half the horizon.

"Over there."

The captain shrugged his shoulders.

"But where were the Germans? Do you know if they've worked round Marville to the south?"

"Mon capitaine, I was in a trench. . . . There was a lot of shelling, great black shells they were. . . . First they burst behind us, a hundred yards away. . . . As long as that went on we weren't worrying. . . . But they started dropping right in among us. . . . And then we cleared out!"

"But your officers?"

He made a gesture of ignorance. There was nothing to be got out of him. At that moment there came the scream of an approaching shell, and the man ducked his head and set off at a run, round-backed, moaning, "Ah! bon Dieu de bon Dieu!"

The shell burst on the far side of the road, and was quickly followed by three more, which fell nearer. The captain was still watching the distant troops, which were on the point of disappearing altogether into the wood. We had gathered round him in a ring, anxiously waiting.

"I believe they're French," he said. "Lintier, you have a look. You've got good eyes."

He handed me his glasses, and at the end of a short scrutiny I was able to make out red trousers.

"Yes, they're French all right. But where are they going?"

The captain made no answer, and I realised that, once more, the French army was in retreat.

Another salvo ploughed up the ground behind us.

The shelling had so far been well to the left and beyond us, but was getting more accurate with each salvo. In direction it was now exactly right. My life depended momentarily on the will of a Prussian captain and a minute change of elevation.

Suddenly some sections of infantry appeared over the edge of the plateau, retiring at the double. A company of the 101st Regiment installed itself in the empty trenches behind our guns.

The air vibrated again as a salvo came straight at us. The earth shot up in great gouts. A splinter shaved my head and rang against the armour plating of the limber. One of the shells had burst in the trench occupied by the infantry. Two slow seconds went by; then came a sound of groans and cries. No movement. Then a man climbed out and ran off, then another, then the whole company, with bowed heads and bent knees, crouching as they ran. A wounded man hurriedly rid himself of his pack and rifle and limped along behind them as fast as he could go.

A mounted orderly came with a message for the major: orders to retire. The Army Corps was in retreat. We limbered up and moved off in column, at a walk. The yellow stubble-field, torn up by the shells and exposing its entrails of dark soil, had something of the horror of a body covered with gaping wounds. Loose clods lay scattered round each of the shell-holes, which had a circular rim of raised earth. We were not yet clear of the danger; death might still descend on us at any moment. Someone asked:

"Why don't we get along more quickly? . . . We'll get smashed to bits. . . ."

But the fact was that fatalism, which I take to be the beginning of courage, had taken hold of us all. We were not in sight of the enemy. His shells were like bolts of fate dropping from the sky. Why here rather than there? That was what neither ourselves nor the enemy could possibly know. So where was the good of hurrying? Death could as easily reach us a little farther off. Why go to the right or left? Useless, utterly useless. . . . At the head of the column our officers rode boot to boot, talking.

A single infantryman was left in the trench where the shell had fallen. He lay on his stomach, on some straw with which the bottom of the trench had been lined. There was a hole in his back. The blood had made a great dark ring round it on the cloth. Another piece of the shell had laid the back of his neck open; his cap had fallen off and his face was thrust forward into the ground. The sight drew all our eyes as we went by. But no one said anything. What was there to say, about a shell that had burst and a man that was dead? . . .

Another defeat. . . . Just like 1870 over again! The thought obsessed our minds and overwhelmed us.

"They're so blasted strong. Look at that," said Déprez to me, with a sweep of his arm indicating line after line of French infantry in full retreat across the plateau, as far as the eye could see. "Six hours of fighting at Latour; not much more to-day. And beaten again. Hell!"

We felt a wave of anger rise in us against the men who had given way. When it had been our own turn on Saturday, by the bowl-shaped tree, we had stood our ground.

A Battery of "Seventy-fives" in action, August 1914.

(From a contemporary drawing.)

In the distance over by Marville columns of artillery were trotting across the level fields. A blue and red squadron raised a cloud of dust. The fluctuation of infantry on the march, growing less distinct, but still perceptible, as far as the horizon . . . the dust of cavalry . . . dark lines of artillery. The sun blazed overhead. The cannonading and all other noise had ceased. Mirage rose from the hot, dry soil and half veiled the great movements of troops. It seemed as if the whole countryside was on the march.

We came to Remoiville, over which towered the noble pile of an early Renaissance castle, grandly simple in its lines and raised on tiers of terraces. A Red Cross flag floated from its topmost turret. In the village there was not a soul to be seen. All the doors and windows were closed. Some chickens were scavenging over a heap of manure; piercing squeals came from a miry sty in which two gunners were cutting the throat of a pig. Otherwise no sign of life until, from the door of one of the last houses—a wretched hovel in the dark interior of which one caught a glimpse of a polished chest of drawers—two old, old women looked out at us with eyes that could hardly be seen beneath their wrinkled, heavy lids. Their fixed, steely gaze seemed to be importuning us reproachfully.

Ah! well we know the sharp remorse of a retreating army. Bitter indeed is the shame in our hearts as we go through these villages we cannot save, leaving them a prey to the relentless enemy. Inanimate things take to themselves the face of human anguish. Abandoned houses confront us with the very lineaments of despair. Mere fancy, no doubt. Imagination! But even as such, most poignant, for to-morrow those houses will be burning, and we, from the hill where we bivouac at night, shall watch the leaping flames.

It seems clear that the Allies have won successes in the North and in Alsace. This is stated in the Army Bulletins which are issued to us from time to time, and also in the Communal Bulletins. If it is so, how shall we support the terrible reproaches of the people and things we are unable to save from an enemy who is too numerous for us?

There was a long delay at Remoiville. A river had to be crossed, and there was only one bridge. The crossing was effected slowly and in perfect order. Then, along a single road, through a country of hills and valleys, cool green forest and fresh meadow-clearings, the retreat of the 4th Corps began.

An imposing line of high hills shut in the western horizon at no great distance, and seemed to offer a position where the army could halt and entrench.

Along the right of the road moved the interminable procession of artillery and wheeled transport: guns of every calibre, limbers, lorries, forage-waggons, regimental carts, divisional ambulances, corps ambulances, and farm-waggons full of pale wounded, many of them wearing turbans of bloodstained lint. Abreast, on the left of the road, the infantry marched in column of fours. The surface of the road very soon became broken and uneven.

Immediately in front of us was a howitzer battery. One of the corporals belonging to it had half a sheep dangling from his saddle.

Our 10th Battery had lost all its guns earlier in the day. The men had been unable to save them when, at about one o'clock, the infantry broke completely; the enemy's fire almost annihilated the teams. Captain Jamain, commanding, was wounded in the side by a shell-splinter, and we now saw him lying in a hay-cart among the infantry wounded.

The dense forest, almost dark in spite of the powerful

sun, muffled the steady tramp of the infantry and the rumbling of the vehicles.

At frequent intervals we passed foundered horses standing stock-still in the ditch by the side of the road, with their heads hanging down and a glassy stare in their half-closed bleary eyes. Sometimes a wheel knocked into them. But they never stirred an inch, and only lay down to die.

The hills in front of us dominated all the plain to our rear, as well as the forest through which we were passing; but it soon became evident that the 4th Corps was not to stand and face the enemy on these heights. Someone told me that the whole of Ruffey's command was retiring behind the Meuse. But while the retreat went on along the main road, our group of artillery turned aside up a side road, which led first to a village full of troops, and thence, with many windings, up a steep, thickly wooded slope.

We began the climb. The sky became rapidly overcast, and drops of rain began to fall. The main road below, along which the interminable procession of troops rolled ever onwards, looked, between the even lines of poplars on either side of it, like a canal of dark water, but a canal with a perceptible current. Our column halted. The wheels had to be securely wedged. The men were tired and silent. The only noise came from the bits as the horses shook their heads, and from the rain splashing on the leaves.

Soon we moved on a few hundred yards, and then halted again on another straight stretch of the steep road. During this halt a country cart came along and tried to pass the column. It was piled with bedding on which, under a great umbrella, sat an old woman and a young woman evidently with child. Several badly wedged waggons had got out of line and barred the way. To drag the overloaded vehicle up the hill there was only a fat mare between the shafts, with a young colt in front which pulled wildly from side to side. A girl was leading the mare by the head, and both she and the beast faced their task with great determination.

"*Allons, hue!*"

The mare bent her back in a mighty effort. With help from the gunners they at length came to the head of the column, from whence onwards the road was clear. There they stopped for a moment's rest. While the girl stood stroking the nostrils of the heavy, smoking animal, we spoke to her.

"Where are you making for?"

"We hardly know, monsieur. We must cross the Meuse, at any rate. . . . And we're behindhand already. All the others of our village started off this morning, as soon as the guns began. But we wanted to see how things would turn out. And then of course we had to come away too. We couldn't have stayed, could we?"

"No," we confessed, "you had to come away."

"Tell me, they're savages, absolute savages, aren't they?"

"Yes."

"They'll burn our houses . . . we shall find nothing left, nothing but ashes. . . . It's dreadful! Oh, why can't you kill them, all of them?"

"Ah, if we only could!"

"Allons, hue! la vieille."

They set off again up the hill.

"Good luck, messieurs!"

"Thanks—good luck to you!"

Before long we, too, moved on. Near the summit we found a wide clearing in the woods, from which point of vantage one saw all the forest draped like a rich mantle over the neighbouring heights, softening and veiling the abrupter ridges; and looking back one could see the whole of the flat plain we had traversed, including

Remoiville and the plateau before Marville, where the line of poplars near which we had been in action in the morning stood out conspicuously in the bald landscape.

In this clearing, in a half-reaped cornfield, it was decided to await the enemy. Our business was to cover the retreat of the 4th Corps, still visibly in progress along the main road below, where now a long line of Paris motor-buses was defiling. The sky was dark; heavy clouds were collecting in the west and promised to cut short the day.

Moving along the side of the wood in order not to disclose its presence, the battery took up a position on the fringe of the forest, behind an outlying clump of smaller trees which sufficiently masked it from in front. The teams and waggons withdrew to a spot where, from a distance, they seemed one with the dark green background. A quiet night seemed probable, though to-morrow might be a different story; for the two batteries of which the brigade now consisted, and which had only seven guns between them, must hold up the enemy long enough to assure the retreat of the main body. But for the present our minds were empty of the morrow; we were too tired to think about it.

The horses had yet to be watered; we took them down an almost perpendicular path to the village below, which was still thronged with troops. Here, through the open window of the mairie, I saw General Boëlle. His expression was grave without being severe. I looked for evidence of anxiety in his face, but found none.

The infantry had piled arms in front of the houses on either side of the street. A flag in its sheath lay across two of the piles. Round the door of the rectory a crowd of at least two hundred men had collected, noisily shaking their water-bottles at arm's length. Word had been passed round that the curé was giving away all his wine. Some chasseurs, with the reins of their chargers over their arms, were waiting for orders. They stood leaning against the wall of the church, close to the water-trough, and I overheard the following conversation:

"So Mortier's dead, eh?"

"Yes, a bullet got him in the stomach."

"Did he say anything?"

"No, simply 'They've got me.' He lay down on the ground with both hands to his stomach . . . and turned over twice. . . . 'Ooh . . . ugh . . . they've got me,' he said. Balthasar, his horse, sniffed at him as he lay there. He hadn't let go of the reins. He held them just as I'm holding mine, over his arm. When Balthasar sniffed at his face he just managed to grunt, 'Poor old brute,' then he seemed to sort of shrivel up, breathing very hard, and then with a last 'Ough . . . ugh!' he suddenly went limp all over. And there was one chasseur the fewer! . . . I closed his eyes; they hadn't a nice look in them at all. And I broke a branch off a tree and put it over his head; it's what I'd like done to me . . . it's only decent when a chap's dead. And after that I came away, leading Balthasar."

When we started on our return journey many of the infantry had marched off. Others were putting on their equipment and unpiling arms. We were told that a single battalion was all we were going to have supporting us. This turned our thoughts to the increasingly ominous prospect of to-morrow's fighting.

An infantry captain hailed Astruc, who was perched on Lieutenant Hély d'Oissel's great charger.

"Hi, there, gunner!"

"Sir!"

"May I be damned if that's not Tortue!"

"Tortue? What's Tortue?"

"Why, my horse that I've lost. There's no doubt about it. Dismount and hand my horse over at once!"

Astruc demurred:

"But this is the lieutenant's horse, sir. I've got to take him back. Good Lord, what'd he say if I went back without him?"

"I tell you to get off! I know my own saddle when I see it. . . . And the beast herself—look, she recognises me. . . . There's no question about it at all, it's Tortue, my mare that I lost at Ethe!"

"But, captain, it isn't a mare at all . . . it's a horse!"

The captain examined the animal.

"God bless my soul! . . . So it is . . . you're right. That's a funny thing. . . . I could have sworn it was Tortue!"

In the deepening twilight the woods surrounding our clearing seem denser, more massive than ever. Another German hawk came over just now, darker against the dark clouds. Can we have been visible? If he saw us, we shall be shelled at dawn to-morrow. He swayed in the sky above the forest, for the wind has freshened and is blowing in sharp gusts from the west.

We have gathered a quantity of the cut corn and spread it round the guns. It will be cold to-night, and most likely wet. The wind shakes our cloaks out and flattens them against our bodies, so that we ourselves seem agitated by it. Over the vast, shadowy void of the plain below, where not a light is to be seen, the muzzles of our guns point menacingly. We have been allowed to make a fire in a corner of the field, where it penetrates deep into the forest, and the almost overhanging trees are like the sides of a sheer black wall. Puffs of wind fan the flames jerkily, making the shadows of the men dance across the ground; sometimes the light is quite extinguished, then it flares up again suddenly. I am worn out. Serving the gun engenders an irresistible need of sleep. I feel rather hungry, but only a little. I can't wait for the meat to be cooked and the coffee boiled. I have eaten a piece of cold bully-beef, and am going now to lie down in the straw under the lee of my limber.

WEDNESDAY, *August 26th.*

We were roused at dawn, to find the battery enveloped in thick mist and our clothes soaked with dew. Our numbed limbs moved unsteadily and slowly. And the first hour of the day, when the light is dim and treacherous, always induces an uneasy, uncomfortable feeling which, being still heavy with sleep, one finds hard to throw off.

As we stood motionless by the guns, wrapped in our cloaks, we had leisure to appreciate our situation in this lonely glade in the midst of the forest. To our right, by our officers' admission, it is quite uncertain whether there are any French troops. And on that side the woods extend without a break from the hill on which we are right down on to the plain, as far as Remoiville. To our left, the 4th Corps should have made good its withdrawal; for we know that, according to the text-books, ten hours is the time normally required by an army corps for this purpose, moving along a single road. Fifteen hours have elapsed since the 4th Corps began its march.

It is very evident that our position, a difficult one in itself, will become dangerous in the extreme unless the mist disperses. Our field of vision only extends a distance of about fifty yards from the guns. The enemy could advance across the plain on to the heels of the retreating army and take us by surprise.

Thus on all sides we have the woods and what they may conceal—the unknown, surprise. In front, the mist and the enemy; behind us the Meuse; danger everywhere.

The Meuse! We are anxious about the Meuse. When the time comes for us to withdraw in our turn, may not the enemy, unopposed on the left, have reached the river before us? Shall we even find a bridge? The necessity of saving the army may mean that we have to be sacrificed.

The hours pass. The mist seems to form on the side of the hills overlooking the Meuse. From there the west wind blows it across the hilltops in trailing clouds which shroud us here as they pass, then drive on down the slope and collect more thickly in the plain.

I am writing these notes on my knee, with my back against the brass bases of the shells in the ammunition-waggon, which is opened for action like a cupboard. We are smoking, waiting.

At last, at about eight o'clock, the sun appeared over the hills; then the mist, hanging like a thick veil before our eyes, began to withdraw. The green landscape became discernible. For a space, white wisps here and there hung about the tops of the tallest trees. Everything was perfectly still. The road, which yesterday had been black with men and horses, now lay absolutely white across the dewy fields, which were touched to a brilliant green by the first gleams of sunshine. Lying flat in the grass in front of our guns, on a sort of natural wooded terrace, among the isolated trees that dotted the downward slope, we stared out across the plain. In the far distance every object in sight seemed to move; it required a determined effort to dispel the illusion.

The men were saying among themselves that we were expected to hold on in our position for two days. Impossible! Someone declared that he had heard the actual instructions given to the major by a general.

"You will hold on," he had said, "as long as the position is tenable. I rely on your skill and instinct as a gunner."

And another voice added:

"Yes, those were his very words. 'Solente, I rely on your skill and instinct as a gunner. . . .' I tell you I heard him with my own ears."

It was also remarked by someone that Saturday's battle would be known as the Battle of Ethe.

"No," asserted another, "it'll be called the Battle of Virton."

"Ethe, Virton . . . what the hell difference does it make? We're out of it; that's all that signifies."

"No, it ought to be settled," declared the trumpeter. "Suppose you're home again and someone asks you where you fought. You say, 'Away over the Belgian frontier.' Yes, but Belgium's a big place! . . . It's a bit bigger than the commune you live in, for instance . . . was it at Liège, or Brussels, or Copenhagen? A silly sort of goat you'd look!"

The goat shrugged his shoulders.

We opened a tin of bully with a bayonet and ate it between four of us. There was nothing to be heard except from where a man was cutting down a small birch tree that obstructed the line of fire of his gun.

The silence was too absolute, the stillness too complete. The enemy was there. We could neither see him nor hear him. So much the more was he to be feared. The utter peacefulness, while we waited for battle, was quite agonising. One's nerves were set on edge.

Surely the 4th Corps must have made good its retreat. . . . The time passed, the French Army receded and receded, the enemy was creeping closer and closer through the woods. . . .

Suddenly, at about two o'clock, we were startled by the rattle of a machine-gun, firing close at hand in the forest. A mounted orderly came galloping across the clearing with a message for the major. The latter immediately ordered up the waggons.

Had our retreat been cut off? The staccato note of the machine-gun was now accompanied by intermittent bursts of rifle-fire. The clearing had to be crossed diagonally to reach a track through the forest. Very calmly, fully determined to save our guns, we got out our carbines and loaded them. But the column crossed the field without our hearing a single bullet. We reached the wood. Haste was essential. Even if the road was still free, it might cease to be in another moment.

Leaning down over the collars of their horses to avoid the low branches that threatened to sweep them from their saddles, and carefully eyeing the narrow passage between the trees, the drivers urged their teams forward with whip and spur.

The road was free. . . . We came to Dun-sur-Meuse, the point where we were to cross the river. The captain summoned the non-commissioned officers:

"The bridge is mined. Warn your drivers to take care of the sacks they will see lying at each side of the roadway. They're full of melinite."

To enable us to cross, the sappers put planks over the trench they had dug in the centre of the bridge.

The hindmost waggons of our column had not advanced two hundred yards beyond the farther bank of the Meuse when a great explosion shook us violently in our seats. The bridge had been blown up. Behind us a vast white smoke-cloud swirled and bellied, blocking out half the town.

While we were waiting for orders, drawn up in a field in double column, a shout went up:

"Here comes the postman!"

"At last!"

"Letters! Letters! One man per gun!"

We had been waiting a week for news from home.

Those who received letters moved apart to read them.

It has been definitely decided to call last Saturday's battle the Battle of Virton.

THURSDAY, *August 27th.*

It rained all the night through and was still raining in the morning. The thought of all the discomfort entailed by such weather took the edge off the satisfaction we should otherwise have felt after more than ten hours' sleep in a warm and comfortable barn. Hooded in horse-rugs which dangled down to our calves behind, we silently emerged in twos and threes on to the muddy road and splashed our way to the field where we had parked the guns.

The horses were standing very still and resigned, with glistening coats, always trying to hold their sterns to the rain. The men on stable-guard had succeeded in lighting fires; they had had to scoop new holes for the purpose, for yesterday's were full of water, with the charred wood-embers floating in it.

Their cloaks were streaming, and sodden and stiff with wet. Some of the men had pulled up their capes over their heads. All now gathered in a ring and held their reddened hands over the flames.

"Curses on this rain! Two days more of it and everyone'll be down with dysentery."

"Which'll do more damage than the shelling," added Hutin.

"What's the good of trying to make coffee?" growled Pelletier; "it's nowhere near hot yet, and won't be for hours at this rate."

"It's the wood; it won't burn properly. It only smokes."

"Blow on it a bit, Millon."

We held the soles of our boots to it to dry them a little. The rain hissed in the flames.

"Well, one thing's certain," remarked the trumpeter, "and that is that if we hadn't been betrayed we need never have retired."

This made me angry.

"Betrayed! I've been expecting some idiot to say that this week past!"

"Oh, you have, have you? Well, it is so, that's all! I was told so yesterday. A general sold the plans to the enemy. I know what I'm talking about, see?"

"What rot!"

"I've heard exactly the same thing," put in another voice.

"Balderdash! It's the sort of damned silly rumour that would be started the moment we get the least knock. . . . If you're beaten, you're betrayed! . . . The French can't be the weaker, of course; that's not possible! Yet you know perfectly well there are five army corps facing us. Two to one, in other words. . . . But that makes no difference. Oh Lord, no. It may be two to one, but we can't be beaten. . . . We must have been betrayed! Then why have you kept on saying that all we need is de Langle de Cary's Army to support us? Eh? . . . Why, simply because you know there aren't enough of us to face the Boches on our own! . . ."

"I say there are traitors," insisted the trumpeter stubbornly; "there always have been and always will be traitors ready to sell France."

"Imbecile!" declared Hutin peremptorily.

Almost all my comrades share my feelings on this question. Given reasonable reinforcements we could gain the ascendancy. And even without them we shall be able to hold the line of the Meuse.

It is only in the days of defeat which we have lived through that we have learnt how deeply a man can love his country. The fulness of the emotion could never be revealed to an immediately victorious army. Men must have striven and suffered, they must have been afraid, if only for the briefest space, of losing their country utterly, before they can know what it means to them. It means all the charm of life, all affections, every joy of eyes, heart and mind. It is what makes life worth living: all this, personified in a single being, a living, suffering being, born of the will of millions of individuals, is France.

To defend her is to defend oneself, since she is, literally, one's raison d'être. Therefore to die is the less bitter alternative, because France beaten would seem worse than death. This is felt by every soldier, either confusedly or in the full glow of consciousness, according to his mind and heart.

Not that any of us speak of it. The very words which, in time of peace, too often smothered the truth beneath their grandiloquence, would be an offence among us now. But the passion, for a passion it is, lies at the very depth of our hearts, dwells there with the intimate, sacred emotions which would be profaned if one gave them expression.

"Harness up and hook in! We're moving!"

The rain had frayed the men's tempers.

"Look out with that great bear of yours! You'll be getting us killed."

Hutin shouted:

"Are you going to take your horses off the line so that

the ropes can be packed up? Oh, you aren't, eh? . . . Right, I'll turn 'em loose myself, then, and to hell with you!"

"There's a fool for you! To go and tie up a horse to a limber-wheel! He's eaten half the oats out of the sack. . . . Pull him out of it!"

Cramone, whipping his pair furiously, repeated for the twentieth time:

"*I'll* teach you manners before I've done with you!"

"What lazy swine left these rations out in the wet last night?" cried Millon.

"*Will* you back those lousy mokes of yours? . . . How the hell am I to get the ropes on? . . . I never saw such a half-baked cuckoo!"

The drivers thrashed and pulled at their horses which, with their heads to the wind, kept shying to right and left to avoid the stinging impact of the rain in their ears. Even Bréjard became wrathful:

"Come on, now, pull yourselves together! Get straightened out, for God's sake! . . . Can't you see that off leader has got a leg over?"

"And they told us we were due for a rest to-day!"

"Are the Boches resting, d'you suppose?"

Getting away was a difficult business. The wheels had sunk deep into the soaking ground during the night, and the horses' hoofs slipped in all directions down the wet slope of the field.

Once on the road the battery broke into a trot, sending up fountains of liquid mud. Some of the men who were suffering from colic had been taken short by the sudden move, and had to hurry after the column fastening up their trousers as they ran.

Our goal was the farther flank of a strong artillery position on the heights overlooking the Meuse. A noise of sharp, intermittent cannonading came to us from the hills in the direction of Stenay. Shrapnel could be seen bursting in the distance, over some woods. It stopped raining, and the sky gradually grew lighter, till it was uniformly white from horizon to horizon.

Some peasants flying before the invasion had encamped for the night in a meadow by the roadside. Their cart had a high green tilt to it, which served them for a tent. Standing in front, an old man and two women, both of them enceinte, with half a dozen children clinging to their skirts, watched us go by.

The road was uphill, and the column slowed to a walk. I heard one of the women say to the old man, nudging him with her elbow:

"Go on, father!"

The old man seemed to hesitate. She was insistent.

"You must!"

Then the good man, evidently much against his will, came over to us. He looked down, coloured, and muttered in a shamefaced way:

"No, I can't do it! How can they expect me to ask such a thing, at my age?"

He was turning to go back, when we questioned him:

"To ask what, old chap?"

"Whether you happen to have a little bread to spare? It's for the children. . . ."

"Why, yes, of course! We never eat it all."

The truth is that we hardly ever have enough. Every loaf needs carefully examining, and by the time the mouldy parts have been removed the ration is generally cut down by half. While the ration-bag was being opened, the old man walked alongside of our limber.

"Here you are!"

We held out two nearly new loaves for him to take.

"With an onion and a tooth or so you'll find it's quite eatable."

"Thank you, thank you! . . . But are you sure this won't leave you short? . . ."

Civilian refugees in Belgium, August 1914.

"No fear; we get cart-loads of the stuff every day!"

The old fellow went off with his loaves under his arm. I saw him shrug his shoulders and wipe his eyes with his sleeve.

A salvo of shrapnel burst over the dark woods in the distance.

"Damn them!" growled Millon, who had given his bread, between his teeth.

And he shook his fist at the enemy.

Having reached our position, covering the right bank of the Meuse, we proceeded to dry ourselves in the sun.

In the afternoon a small body of horsemen, uhlans, no doubt, appeared on the edge of a distant wood. A well-directed salvo sent them hurrying back again.

FRIDAY, *August 28th.*

"Stand to!"

"What's that?"

"Stand to! Come on, up you get!"

"What time is it?"

"Don't know. It's pitch-dark still."

"Right, up's the word! Wake up, Hutin!"

I shook my comrade, who growled out:

"All right, all right! Hell, but I was comfortable!"

The barn filled with the noise of shifted straw.

"What time is it?" the same voice repeated.

"Look out, up there! There's a gap in the ladder."

Feet scraped clumsily down the rungs. A man rapped out an oath.

"Get the lantern!"

"Where is it?"

"Hanging behind the door."

The men groped about in the dark for their equipment.

"Where's my cap?"

"I can't find the lantern. Come and help look for it."

"I bet it's not more than two o'clock!"

"Come on, look sharp now!" shouted a sergeant, looking in at the door. "Is everyone awake?"

No one answered. The air outside was keen. The night was pitch-dark, without a star. The infantry were already paraded. They had lit fires in the street, and their coffee was almost ready for them. The wretched little church, lit up from below by the fires, loomed like a vast cathedral. Its weathervane was lost in the upper darkness; fantastic shadows danced on the walls, and gleams of red and green came and went in the stained-glass windows. Many unfortunate refugees had crowded into the church for the night, together with a number of soldiers who had been unable to find a billet elsewhere. The nave, seen through the open door, presented a strange appearance, full of flickering lights which produced a disturbing effect, as if a fire had broken out. Gleams from the coloured windows showed vague, human forms stretched on the stone floor. Outside, in the central square of the village, the infantrymen moving back and forth in front of their fires cast huge shadows along the ground and up the walls.

What was the meaning of this sudden alarm? Had the enemy succeeded in crossing the frontier by Stenay? We moved off in rear of the infantry, whose innumerable tramp suggested a migrating herd. One felt a million presences in the night, a vast breathing of humanity, a muffled undernote of voices; all the invisible life and movement sent forth fluid waves through the dark night air.

From the distance, in the direction in which we were marching, came the noise of gun-fire.

Soon the first hint of day glimmered, disclosing the sombre outline of the rich, wooded hills between us and the Meuse. One looked down on the village of Tailly in a ravine below the road: a few huddled houses, a church tower, a cemetery.

The cold immobility of the dawn by little and little gave way to the infinite vibration of the light over field and forest. Then, through a gap between the hills, the road dropped steeply down to the river.

When we arrived at Beauclair, in the valley of the Meuse, the action seemed to be over.

There were rows of piled arms in the square in front of the church, and beside them, on the bare ground, lay the infantry who had been fighting. Most of them looked pale, though here and there one noticed very red faces. They lay perfectly still. The rigid masks of the sleepers expressed an exhaustion that was tragic. Unbuttoned coats and shirts revealed bare chests. They were all muddy; their trousers were plastered with dirt up to the knees.

The battery halted opposite the last houses of the little town, and the cooks proceeded at once to prepare coffee. A giant of an infantryman came to beg an onion of us, and we asked him about the fight.

"They didn't manage to get across the Meuse, then?"

"Yes, a brigade of them did . . . but the artillery destroyed the bridges behind them. . . . And we drove them back into the river with the bayonet. Ah, you gunners, you don't know what a charge is like! It's a bloody nightmare. . . . If there's such a thing as hell, it must be a place where there's always bayonet-fighting going on. . . . Seriously, I mean it. You start off, shouting . . . one or two men get hit and drop down, then a whole lot more . . . and the fewer there are left, the louder you have to shout, to keep yourself going. And then, when you get there, you just lose control . . . go at them like mad. . . . I tell you, the first time you feel your bayonet in a man's stomach it does something. . . . It's soft ; you only have to shove it in. . . . It's getting it out again that's the job! . . . I was so clumsy that I pinned one of them to the ground, a great fat chap with a red beard. I couldn't get my bayonet out of him. Had to put my foot on his belly and pull. I could feel him squirm under my foot. Look here, look at this. . . ."

He drew his bayonet from its scabbard. It was red up to the hilt. As he walked away he pulled up a tuft of grass to wipe it with.

The hours passed. It became more and more unlikely that the enemy would renew his attempts to cross the Meuse before to-morrow.

There was a rumour at Beauclair that d'Amade had delivered a flank attack against the army opposite us, and had retaken Marville.

D'Amade! D'Amade at last! But was it true?

We moved into billets at Halles, two kilometres from Beauclair, at the foot of some high hills. After a long silence gun-fire began again. The enemy bombarded the crest of the hills above us, firing over our heads.

A spacious barn had been allotted us for the night. But at dusk, when we went there to turn in, we found a large party of infantry in possession, and our straw entirely monopolised by them, their packs and their rifles.

At first the gunners were indignant.

"The place is all full of foot-sloggers! There's not an inch of room left!"

But it was a question of squeezing in somehow.

The barn had an upper storey, reached by a ladder. The floor of this loft was badly worm-eaten, but there was enough hay to make it reasonably comfortable.

"That's that, then! Artillery on top, infantry below, as usual. We'll manage. Only try not to shift the ladder."

"Look out with those feet of yours, blast it!"

"How was I to know there was anything in the straw?"

"Now then, up you go!"

The gunners climbed up the ladder four or five at a time. It bent under their weight. An infantryman stood at the foot holding a candle.

"Hey! Keep clear of my nose with your spurs, will you?"

"Look alive now, get along up!"

"The floor's giving way! We shall go through!"

"Go on up, will you? It's better than shells, anyway!"

"Shove up a bit, for God's sake, or the place'll never hold us all."

"Hi, don't go there! There's a hole . . . you'll be falling through on to the foot-sloggers."

Audible complaints now rose from the infantry below.

"Aren't you ever going to settle down up there, gunners? We can't sleep with that row going on! And you're shaking the straw down on us in mouthfuls."

"That's the style; with your mouths full you'll be kept quiet!"

"Get off my stomach."

"I can't see a thing! Bring the lantern up!"

An occasional shell still burst in the distance. I wondered whether to remove my spurs and leggings. It would be much more comfortable. But in case of an alarm I might not be able to find them in the straw. . . . I kept them on, and my revolver-holster also, though it stuck into my side. Then, drawing my chin-strap tight so as not to lose my cap, I composed myself as well as possible for sleep.

SATURDAY, *August 29th.*

Urgent orders to move roused us at two o'clock in the morning. Word went round that the Germans had crossed the Meuse. Yet our artillery must have had the exact range of the river everywhere, and there had been no sound of gun-fire. It was unbelievable.

In the night the road seemed yellow among blue fields. I recognised the yews of a cemetery in which, when we passed it yesterday, a burial had been in progress.

We halted in column on the steep ridge above Tailly, and waited for orders. Meanwhile, the daylight spread across the sky from behind the hills.

One by one the regiments of the 7th Division emerged from the ravine and marched past us up the hill. The men seemed harassed. Their eyes were hollow; the faces of the youngest were yellow, dejected, deeply furrowed; their mouths hung down at the corners. Bent forward under the weight of their heavy load, in the attitude of Christ bearing His cross, the infantrymen climbed the hill as if it had been a calvary. They stopped every hundred yards or so to hitch up their packs with a jerk of the hips. Some of them were swinging their rifles like pendulums to help them forward. Several as they passed us complained of having had nothing to eat for two days. A man of the 101st, a tall, emaciated fellow with feverish eyes, halted by us. He stroked the barrel of the gun.

"Ah," he said to Hutin, "it'd be a kindness on your part if you'd put a shell into my stomach. At least that'd be the end of it all!"

"You ought to be ashamed," answered the layer.

The man made a vague gesture, shrugged his shoulders, and went on, dragging his feet heavily.

When the infantry had all gone by we moved into position on the plateau, at the edge of the woods behind which the line regiments were retiring.

I had heard the major repeat the orders he had received to the captain, namely, to prevent the enemy from gaining a foothold on the plateau. And he had been told, further, "There are now no French troops in front of you."

"So we've got to cover the retreat again, eh? A foul job," declared Millon, the firing-number, a stout-hearted little Parisian with the face of a girl. "We're in as much danger here from rifles and machine-gun bullets as we are from shells. Look at that damned wood over there on the edge of the plateau, beyond that big poplar. There's nothing to stop the devils getting that far, and they'll stick a lot of machine-guns there without our being able to see them, which'll save them the trouble of having to advance across the open. . . . What d'you suppose'll happen to us then? Still, that's what we're here for, no doubt! . . ."

"If the army hadn't been sold things'd be going differently," growled Tuvache, a Breton farm-hand who is brave enough under fire but whose morale is bad.

And he added, being always obsessed with his idea of betrayal:

"What proves it is that they've got across the Meuse without the least difficulty."

Bréjard proceeded to silence him:

"You're worse than the rest, with your eternal talk about betraying. The fighting's going on from the North Sea to Belfort; how can you judge by what happens in one wretched little corner? For all you know we may be letting them advance in order to envelop them later. But there are always some people who know better than the generals. . . . Besides, all this time the Russians are advancing. . . . Do your job and don't grouse . . . we shall stop them in the end, and then they'll get what's coming to them."

Meanwhile we waited for the heads of the enemy columns to emerge at any moment from the valley about Tailly.

The plateau basked in that utter stillness, broken only

by the sparkle of the dew, which heralds a day of exceptional heat.

Four black, isolated points appeared in the distance on the road. Was it the German advance-guard? No. They soon became recognisable as three stragglers and a cyclist. Then a body of infantry emerged from the valley, marching in column of fours. In such formation these could still not be the enemy. They proved to be a battalion of the 101st, and passed on and disappeared down the road behind the woods. But soon afterwards, in the folds of the broad, undulating downs which extended to the north-west as far as the dark mass of a distant forest, Lieutenant Hély d'Oissel made out through his glasses, indistinctly because of the dust, great masses of men marching westwards. Was it the enemy? Or were they the French troops which had occupied the heights overlooking the Meuse towards Stenay and were now retiring?

We had already experienced the same terrible uncertainty at Marville. The captain climbed up an apple tree to obtain a better view. The major, too, stared and stared through his glasses. Neither could decide the vital question. A haze, the moisture of the night evaporating in the sun, was beginning to rise from the ground, and obscured the distant view. If they were enemy columns they would endanger the flank of the retreating army. A scout had galloped off to reconnoitre as soon as they were noticed. Time passed; the columns receded westwards. At last the scout returned: they were French. He had recognised the troops of chasseurs acting as flank-guards to the infantry.

We resumed our watch for the enemy, standing motionless in the dewy grass.

Towards the middle of the day we were ordered forward to the edge of the plateau, behind a mask of trees, with instructions to watch the Tailly ravine and the hills south of Stenay. And we had hardly moved into our new position before the infantry regiments came out of the forest, deployed, and went on ahead of us.

"I wish I knew what was happening!" said Hutin to me.

"So do I."

It was hot. We were thirsty and our water-bottles were empty.

Twilight found us still waiting, with still no sign of the enemy.

When it was quite dark we moved away to the other side of the wood to bivouac.

The moon rose above the forest. The noise of the horses' hoofs and the monotonous rumble of the vehicles had a pleasant, soothing effect. The road was smooth and hardly jolted us at all. No one spoke. We were all dozing and dreaming. It only needs such an hour of secure, lazy peacefulness, in the evening after a day on the watch or in action, to make all the miseries of war endurable without complaint.

There was no sound in the warm night but that of the moving column. Our minds were busy with fond memories and dreams of the past. One forgot the dangers and toils of the present; one wandered far afield in space and time. Lyon, in the evening . . . the great lines of light along the quays and their reflections in the Rhone. . . . Above the river the amphitheatre of La Croix-Rousse, the twinkling lights and, high over all, the stars. Impossible to say where the city ends, where the sky begins. And the Mayenne, on lovely autumn and summer days, with its dark water and rich reflections. . . . I saw the ripples widening behind my boat, disturbing the unsubstantial world of the reflections.

And to-morrow I might be dead.

As if I had myself been able to write them, I felt all the melancholy nostalgia of these lovely lines of du Bellay:

Quand reverrai-je, hélas ! de mon petit village
Fumer la cheminée, et en quelle saison
Reverrai-je le clos de ma pauvre maison,
Qui m'est une province et beaucoup davantage ?

I repeated the lines several times to myself under my breath.

SUNDAY, *August 30th.*

In the morning, a long march in clouds of dust. The sun scorched the back of our necks. We were thirsty, and the dust got into our throats so that we spat mud. In a narrow ravine where the battery halted outside a village, Villers-devant-Dun (I think), the noise of gun-fire seemed to come as much from the south and west as from the north and east. This at first surprised and then alarmed us. One of the drivers, Janvier, repeated for the twentieth time:

"That's done it; we're surrounded!"

He was haunted by this thought. But we soon realised that a strong echo had created the illusion. Actually the fighting was chiefly confined to the neighbourhood of Dun-sur-Meuse.

We took advantage of the halt to run to the village drinking-fountain. The latest Communal Bulletin was posted up there. First of all we drank great mouthfuls of fresh water, at least a pint apiece. Then we read. All going well! It was curious, though, to learn that Mulhouse had been recaptured, when we never knew it had been lost. We have been discussing the news among ourselves:

"Well, Hutin, what d'you think of it?"

Hutin answered without conviction:

"Not bad. . . . But they don't say anything about our own affair of last week."

Bréjard, the incurable optimist, explained:

"Virton and Marville don't signify at all on so wide a front. Doubtless there are points here and there where we've given ground. But everywhere else all's going well!"

"The sickening thing is to be at the points where all isn't going well."

"It'll change. We're going to get support. They say de Langle isn't more than a day's march away."

"He'd better hurry if he wants to find any of the 4th Corps infantry left!"

True enough. Our line regiments, particularly those of the 8th Division, have suffered terribly. Certain battalions are reduced to a third of their strength. Since Virton many of the companies have been as low as fifty or eighty rifles, and have lost all their officers. Make haste, make haste, de Langle!

In ever-increasing dust, under a blazing sun that seemed to weigh on one's shoulders, we returned along roads we had already traversed to our yesterday's position above Tailly. Thus we had wasted seven hours travelling round in a wide loop.

Almost immediately a German aeroplane flew over. It's a subjection! When these hawks hover above us we feel exactly like frightened sparrows. The enemy has perfected his aerial arm to the degree of virtuosity, and unfortunately our seventy-fives are almost useless against them. We try to manage by digging a hole for the trail, so as to give a sufficient elevation, but by the time the hole has been dug the bird has flown.

This particular aeroplane spotted one of our batteries on the heights overlooking the river, and dropped a flare as an indication to the German artillery. But the battery at once moved away into another position. Shells are now bursting along the crest which it had occupied, monstrous high-explosive shells that shake the ground within a radius of several kilometres and blur the green landscape with their noisome smoke-clouds.

"Those'll be some of their famous 9-inch howitzers," the captain observed.

We have nothing to do. The horizon towards Stenay is motionless and deserted. For hours now the great shells have been dropping in salvos of three, making dark holes in the unoccupied green meadow across the valley. We are in their line of fire, and they have only to lengthen range a little to drop right among us; but we are not bothering about it.

I am filled with wonder at the marvellous faculty of adaptation which is at the base of human nature, and at the ease with which men accustom themselves alike to danger, the worst privations and continual uncertainty as to the morrow.

Before the war, I remember, I used to ask myself how old people, who have arrived at the extreme limits of existence, can live quite calmly in the very shadow of approaching death. Now I understand. The risk of death has become, for us, a normal element of our every-day existence. Once it is taken into account in this way it ceases to surprise and is robbed of much of its terror. Moreover, each successive day adds something to our stock of courage; the human beast, as it becomes familiarised with the same dangers, flinches less with each experience. Nerves grow steadier; the conscious and continuous effort towards self-mastery becomes more and more effective. That is the whole secret of military bravery. One isn't born brave; one becomes brave. Resistance against the universal instinct to win is merely more or less stubborn in different individuals. And a man must live, as much on active service as elsewhere; he is forced to accommodate himself to the new mode of existence, however hazardous and unpleasant it may be. Well, the most unpleasant element in it, which indeed makes it intolerable at first, is fear, the strangle-hold of fear. Fear, therefore, must be overcome; and overcome it is.

Besides the need of living as little ill as possible, a sense of duty and a wholesome respect for the opinion of others —in a word, honour—plays the chief part in the making of a soldier. This is no new discovery, of course; it is simply a conclusion reached by personal observation.

I fully recognise, be it added, that learning to be brave is a much easier process for us than for the infantry, who are the most disinherited of all the combatants. A gunner, under fire, simply cannot run away; the whole battery would see him; his shame would be patent and beyond repair. It seems to me that fear, in its worst form, is more than anything else an utter loss of will-power. And the man who is incapable of nerving himself to face danger will also be incapable, in most instances, of making up his mind to the horrible shame of open flight. To run away in such circumstances he would need will-power, he would even need a kind of courage. The infantryman, on the other hand, is most often isolated in battle. If he is lying four yards away from the next man, under a hot fire, he is alone. Consideration for himself may well absorb all his faculties. And thus he may yield to the temptation of stopping where he is, or crawling unobserved into some place of safety, or getting lost on purpose, and finally running away. And at nightfall, finding his way back to his platoon, he can explain that he got separated from his section, and has been fighting in another part of the field. He will very likely not be believed, and may be aware of that beforehand. But at least he will not have undergone the abysmal shame of running away in full view of his comrades.

It is something, and not a little either, merely to stay in your place under fire. But to keep cool in the hell of a modern battle is another matter. At the beginning you are afraid, you sweat and tremble: that's irresistible. Death seems inevitable. The danger is an unknown quantity, magnified by imagination. You don't reason about it. The explosion and the acrid smoke are as much a part of the initial terror as the actual shrapnel or fragments of high-explosive shell. Yet neither the flash of the melinite, nor the noise, nor the smoke are dangers; it is simply that they accompany the danger, and you are at first overwhelmed by them all at once; later, you discriminate. The smoke is harmless; the screech of the approaching shell is a useful warning of its direction. You no longer crouch unnecessarily, and only take cover when there is a real risk. The danger, in a word, no longer dominates you; you dominate it. That's the great thing.

To get a perfectly clear notion of the effects of a shell, I went with Hutin to a field of tall Jerusalem artichokes where one, a very large one, had fallen. It had made a crater of some ten yards' diameter in the middle of the field. Only a shell from a howitzer, with a very steep trajectory, could have made so regular a hole. The projectile, falling almost perpendicularly, penetrates far into the ground. When it bursts, it displaces huge masses of earth. Many fragments of steel are buried in the depths of the soil, and the actual danger-zone is proportionately reduced.

We easily verified this. The farther one moved away from the crater, the higher from the ground-level were the artichokes lopped off. At a distance of ten paces only the heads of the tallest were damaged. It followed that a man lying flat quite close to the point of impact would have been untouched. Beyond ten paces a circular zone had been entirely spared. Beyond that again, here and there, leaves and occasionally stalks had been cut by falling fragments, and in this area one would have been about equally exposed whether one lay flat or stood upright.

Viewed in this light, a shell loses much of its moral effect.

Another circumstance that helps the gunner to be brave is the organisation of his branch of the service. The infantryman, the cavalryman and the sapper are units. In our case the unit is the gun. The seven men that serve it are the closely knit, interdependent organs of a being that has life: the gun in action.

This linking of seven men to each other, and of each of them to the gun, makes any failure more patent, grosser in its consequences, more thoroughly disgraceful. Moreover, in such close physical and psychological contact influences are easily felt; one or two stout hearts, sticking to their posts, will often suffice to stiffen the backbones of a whole section.

The day drew to a close in perfect stillness. Neither towards Tailly nor Stenay was there any sign of the enemy.

At dusk we moved away again to the other side of the woods to bivouac. It was a marvellous summer twilight. The road led straight through the deep gloom of the forest into an east that was richer in colours than an immense rainbow.

All noise of battle had ceased. Gradually the light faded; night came on, and there remained, as yesterday, only the low monotonous rumble of the wheels, in the gloom, through the silent woods.

A nocturnal glow from the sky, where the stars were disappearing one by one behind a rising mist, bathed all the mass of the forest, which, from the highest point of the road, could be seen stretching endlessly away like a great fleece into the infinite obscurity. But the darkness under the trees was absolute; the road might have been a trench hollowed out of the very bosom of the earth, had one not seen here and there, glowing strangely through the dark, the still ruddy embers of an infantry bivouac fire, and had not moist scents of mint and other herbs come to us out of the shadowy green depths, mingled with lascivious odours of wild animals. A keen, delicious freshness enveloped us, to which we yielded with a grateful shudder, inhaling it in deep breaths.

Millon, sitting beside me on the limber, told me the story of his life: a sad, simple little tale of himself, only twenty years old, with his girl's face and humorous, childish eyes, having long been the sole support of his family, and of how his mother, his "old woman," as he called her with most loving fervour, was now left alone in Paris with another child, still very young, and nervous and weak so that he is never free from anxiety about her; of past sorrows that he has never forgotten; of the doubts and anxieties they must be going through at present, and their material cares.

"If only my 'old woman' could see me now here, in this peace and quiet! . . ."

In the field where we eventually halted to bivouac we had practically to fight for a few armfuls of straw. The men of a battery which had got there before us were lying about in the deep sleep of exhaustion on a haystack which they had pulled to pieces and spread over the ground. They had twenty times as much straw as they needed. But when we pulled a few trusses from under them, and so woke them up, their exasperation was terrible. They shouted, swore and threatened. But in the end they sank back into sleep, snarling under their breath like vicious dogs.

MONDAY, *August 31st.*

It was still early when the noise of gun-fire roused us. We at once got under way and were back at Tailly by seven o'clock.

We were told that the enemy had been pushed back as far as the Meuse during yesterday's fighting, and that Beauclair and Halles were in our hands again.

In column, in the village, we waited for orders. The German artillery was bombarding the neighbouring heights.

There was a hay-cart in the square with three wounded uhlans in it. A medical officer was walking to and fro in front of the cart with his hands behind his back, and a group of women and children stood silently by, contemplating the Germans. Some of our men went over out of curiosity to look at them; the uhlans gazed back with troubled, melancholy blue eyes.

Tuvache declared:

"They're not such nasty-looking devils as I should have thought."

"I suppose you expected them to have a supplementary eye in the middle of their foreheads," commented Millon, "like the inhabitants of the moon?"

Tuvache shrugged his shoulders:

"No, only I thought they'd be uglier. They don't look so bad as all that."

Heavy fighting developed by the gap in the hills at Beauclair, where the enemy was trying to force a passage. The confused, tremendous roar of the battle, as of a heavy surf breaking over rocks, was continuous.

"En avant! Trot!"

But we had not advanced three hundred yards along the Beauclair road when we were halted again. There were many casualties coming back from the fighting, men with wounds in the hands, arms and shoulders. All were bandaged. Many of them stopped to ask us for a drink of water or a cigarette.

"Are we advancing?" we asked one of them.

"Neither one thing nor the other at present," he answered. "It's those damned machine-guns of theirs!"

"D'you feel much pain?"

"No."

"What's the effect of a bullet wound like that?"

"Burns a bit, that's all. Nothing to speak of."

Men with leg wounds now began to arrive. These were suffering. They were sweating with exertion and heat, for the sun, which was now at its zenith, beat straight down on the narrow valley along which the road wound. Several had cut sticks from the hedgerows to help themselves along with.

One infantryman, with his thigh shattered by a shell, came by on an officer's charger led by a stretcher-bearer. He was clinging to the horse's mane with both hands; his right leg hung loose. From a rent in the trousers, a little above the knee, a stream of blood ran down to the end of the boot, and from there dripped on to the ground. The man's eyes were closed. His violet eyelids, pale lips and long, bony, red-bearded mask put one in mind of a crucifixion.

"Can you manage to hold out?" the stretcher-bearer asked him.

"Are we getting near the ambulance yet?"

"It's quite close now. If you feel yourself falling off, mind you sing out, and I'll get you down. . . . Feeling bad?"

"Yes, it's bleeding such a lot. Look at it on the ground."

"Well, just stick it a bit longer. . . . Hang on tight, now."

An ambulance came past, full of badly wounded men. Instead of being laid at full length they were crowded up with their backs to the sides, so as to get as many in as possible. In the shade of the green canvas hood I could see a lolling, bloodless head, and another that was entirely covered with blood. A tall, dark giant of a corporal was sitting in front by the driver. He held himself perfectly upright, looking very grave and determined, with his rifle between his knees and a hand on one hip; his head was swathed in a bright red bandage, like a turban. The blood had run down into his left eye, which looked strangely white against the red socket, and from there down his drooping moustache and matted beard, and thence in great daubs and splashes on to his broad chest.

A wounded man who had been waiting by the side of the road for some time, sitting on the bank, caught hold of the vehicle as it went by and was dragged along in its wake.

"Stop a bit and let me get in!"

"Sorry, old man, there's no more room!"

"I can't walk any farther."

"But there isn't an inch to spare. You can see!"

"Let me sit on the step!"

"If you can manage it. . . ."

A gunner helped the man to hoist himself on to the step of the still moving vehicle.

In a sunken road, under the shade of some tall poplars, two medical officers had improvised a kind of operating-table on trestles. Many wounded men lay or sat with their backs against the bank, waiting their turn to be attended to. A tiny stream ran faintly trickling over the pebbles at the edge of the road, its waters bloodstained and its course half blocked up with red bandages and cotton-wadding. The air reeked with chemicals and human flesh, and with the natural moist smell of the spring.

Two men brought along a captain whose broken arms hung down helplessly on each side of the stretcher. A medical orderly cut away the sleeves of his tunic. He looked strange, lying on the table with his bare red arms and his torso encased in the tight blue tunic. He sighed deeply while his wounds were being attended to.

"Into line, right wheel!"

Moving across fields up a steep slope, we took up a position on the heights commanding the Beauclair gap and the road we had just left.

A spur ran down between this position and Tailly, hiding all of the latter except the weathercock on the church, which seemed to rise out of the ground.

Through the V-shaped gap in the hills overlooking the Meuse the enemy could see us without difficulty. And we in turn had a view of the woods and meadows beyond Beauclair which he occupied, and which a French battery in front of us, but under cover of another spur, was bombarding with shrapnel.

In the distance the German infantry began debouching across the fields from the woods, looking like an army of black insects on a smooth green lawn. We at once opened fire, and the enemy hastily withdrew back into the woods, which we continued to bombard.

It looked as if the battle as a whole was going in our favour. More French batteries went forward along the Beauclair road and unlimbered in the gap itself. Others moving into position at various points on the hills round about us, and still others farther away on the heights directly overlooking the Meuse, thundered without respite. Clouds of dust and flashes of flame here and there in the green landscape revealed the existence of invisible guns at many points. So violent was the bombardment from this formidable position that the air gradually became thick. An acrid fog of dust and powder floated across the valley; crashing echoes reverberated from side to side and went rolling round the hills; a vast, deafening roar drummed in our ears, overwhelmed us, made us drowsy.

"Cease fire!"

At once all was absolutely still round the guns. It was about midday.

Suddenly, without any preliminary ranging, the enemy began a heavy bombardment of Tailly and the fir woods immediately above our position. Some artillery waggons which had been drawn up at the edge of these woods since morning cleared off at a gallop. A section of infantry emerged out of the smoke of a big high-explosive shell.

"Take cover!" came Captain de Brisoult's word of command.

The fire of the French batteries little by little died down.

Higher up the valley, where our own waggons were waiting, a salvo of shrapnel burst: a fuse went droning loudly through the air. No one seemed to be hit. The waggons still stood there, a motionless dark rectangle on the green grass.

The enemy found the exact range of a battery on the far side of a fir plantation just below us. We watched them getting their guns away one by one through the wood under an inferno of shelling.

Hutin, who was crouching behind the shield, suddenly got up and looked ahead. He stood with folded arms.

"It's begun!" he growled between clenched teeth.

"What's begun? Get down!"

I pulled his sleeve.

"It's begun! The retreat! Ah, bon Dieu de bon Dieu!"

I stood up too. He was right. We could see sections of infantry coming back over the crest.

Bréjard shouted at us:

"Get down under cover, you two!"

A shell burst close by; the pieces whizzed through the air, and a shower of clods and stones spattered the ground all round us. I crouched down instinctively; Hutin never moved, being too preoccupied with the spectacle of the retiring infantry, who were appearing in greater numbers every moment.

"Ah, I thought as much!" he said; "here comes a staff officer; we'll be off too, in a moment. . . . Good God, if we're always going to be retiring like this we might as well take the train while we're about it!"

He was right again: the officer brought us orders to retire at once. Our teams came up the steep hill at a trot. The moment was a perilous one, and as ill-luck would have it, No. 1 gun, which had been backed up against the side of the hill, began running down the slope as soon as we had worked the trail loose from where the recoil had embedded it in the ground. It carried us with it for some yards. Eight men had all they could do to stop it, and there still remained the business of getting it limbered up. The drivers fumed, and the maddened horses pulled and reared in all directions as they were slowly backed towards the gun.

"Now then, all together! . . . One, two, three . . . heave! One, two, three . . . heave!!"

We put our last ounce of strength into one mighty effort. Ah! Got it!

"No. 1 gun ready!"

The team set off at a gallop.

Beyond Tailly the road leading up to the plateau became very steep, particularly where it ran along the low stone wall of the cemetery.

There were some infantry resting beside their piled

arms and equipment on either side of the road. Sitting in the grass, they watched us as we came by with the dull, absent look in their eyes of men who had just come out of the fighting. And suddenly, the screech of its arrival having been drowned by the noise of our wheels, a shrapnel burst right over the cemetery. Some of the infantrymen flung themselves down in the ditch; others flattened themselves against the wall, shielding their heads with their packs. Two men ridiculously stood where they were and hid their heads in the thick foliage of the hedge. We on the limbers ducked and hunched up our shoulders while the drivers urged the teams on with whip and spur.

The next instant we saw that the road ran for some distance in full view of the enemy. It was too late to do anything except make a dash for it.

A salvo. . . . Too far! And we were past the danger-zone.

We went on up the hill and reoccupied our yesterday's position, covering the neighbouring slopes, with the edge of a row of tall poplars as an aiming point. The 3rd Battery, which had been with us on Saturday, had dug some good trenches on this spot. But the waggons had hardly had time to withdraw to the edge of a little wood a short distance away when high-explosive shells began falling all round us.

How could the enemy have spotted our position so quickly? We were thoroughly "defiladed." There was no direction from which we could be observed. We had not fired a single round, so there had been no dust or flashes to give us away. Nor had any aeroplane flown over. What was the explanation? . . .

We took cover in the trenches.

"It's not us they're shooting at," declared Hutin.

"Oh, really? They're shooting at the Pope, perhaps?"

"No, they've seen those four damned squadrons of

dragoons. That's what we owe this to. . . . They've got the road under observation."

But the dragoons receded into the distance and the enemy went on bombarding us. There could be no doubt about it: he must know that there was a battery there. Was there a spy signalling to him from some place of concealment behind us? I looked everywhere but could discover nothing.

Three or four shells fell within a yard or two of the guns, enveloping the whole battery in a cloud of dust and smoke, and shaking us as we lay in the bottom of our trenches. I heard the major's voice shout:

"Get the men under cover to the right!"

While the captain and the lieutenant remained at their observation-post, the men scattered across the field out of the line of fire. But looking back as we ran, I was enraged to see a general and his staff come riding along the road in full view of the enemy. Were we to be killed on their account? There were about twenty officers with the general, who was a little, thin, grey-haired man, lost in an immense cavalry cloak; a troop of chasseurs, in their conspicuous red and blue, followed behind. . . . The air became loud with the scream of another salvo. The chasseurs and the officers turned away their heads and ducked; the little general alone never faltered for an instant. This time the enemy fired short.

"Take post!"

The captain believed he had spotted the battery which was bombarding us. He called:

"Layers to me!"

Feverishly, while the shells still burst all round, the elevation and range were adjusted and we made ready to fire.

"Distribute 15 degrees. No. 1 gun, one hundred and fifty degrees right. . . . No. 2, one hundred and sixty-five degrees. . . . No. 3 . . ."

The fuse-setters repeated the corrector and the range.

"Sixteen. . . . Three thousand five hundred. . . ."

"By threes, from the right, battery fire. . . ."

"No. 1 gun . . . Fire! . . . No. 2 gun . . . Fire! . . . No. 3 . . ."

The action electrified us. In the din made by all the guns firing simultaneously, orders had to be bellowed. We no longer heard the noise of the enemy shells bursting; our own noise completely drowned it; one took no notice of the splinters and shrapnel bullets that were still whizzing all round and overhead.

Very soon the enemy's fire died down, and before long stopped altogether.

"We're on to them!" said Hutin, busy with his dial sight

"Fire!"

"Ready!"

"Fire!"

On the plateau behind us we could see companies of infantry retiring in extended order.

Evening came. We in turn received our orders to retire. It was as if the earth and woods absorbed what was left of the light. The movements of the infantry in the distance were gradually lost in the undulating landscape. The men became one with the fields, dissolved, vanished utterly.

By the edge of a dark shell-hole I saw a red smear. An infantryman lay there, stretched on his back. The shell had blown one of his legs off. By way of the mangled stump, where there was a congealed mass of earth, clover-leaves and gore, he had bled to death. He had bent his head back in his death-agony, so that the Adam's apple stuck up out of the distended neck-muscles. The troubled eyes of the dead man were wide open; his lips absolutely white. He was still grasping his shattered rifle; his cap had rolled on to his shoulder.

TUESDAY, *September 1st.*

It must have been one in the morning when, after a seemingly endless march through the night, we at last halted. Soup had still to be made, and the horses watered and fed, after which we flopped down and went to sleep like dead men.

At four o'clock the corporal of the guard roused us, shaking us awake one by one. Tired, angry growls came from all sides.

"Stand to!"

"This is the limit! We haven't had an hour's sleep."

To keep one's eyes open was almost agony. Our arms and legs were stiff, our heads heavy, our backs aching. It was cold and misty.

We hooked in and moved off.

Numbness and torpor crept from our feet to our knees, invaded our whole bodies. Our heads lolled from shoulder to shoulder. One sank down, down into the nothingness of sleep. Some of the drivers slept in their saddles. They leaned gradually farther and farther to one side, then, just as they were on the point of falling off, woke by instinct and straightened themselves. A moment later one saw their vague outline through the mist, swaying again as before.

Where were we going? Perhaps the army had been compelled to withdraw behind Verdun, because the enemy, who had certainly obtained a foothold on the left bank of the Meuse towards Stenay, was threatening its left flank? We knew nothing; we were too tired to think or even to fear. . . . We would have given our souls for a day's sleep.

In the morning we were halted near Landres, and turned aside off the road into a plum orchard. Unless new orders arrived, we were told, we should rest here for the day.

Fires were lit; we shook down plums from the trees.

A voice called:

"Letters!"

A great savage yell went up in response. The men flung themselves in a body on the post-corporal.

News at last! Some of the letters were dated a fortnight back; ours had not been received. The anxiety of the people at home must be terrible.

When we had read our correspondence through Hutin called to me:

"Come and do some washing."

"Right."

We hung our coats up on the low branches of the plum trees, and with our shirts over our arms and the upper part of our bodies bare except for our braces, went down to the stream at the foot of the orchard.

There we found a little roofed-in washhouse. We knelt down at the edge of the water. Three young girls were similarly employed on the farther bank, just opposite us. One of them was washing a garment with blood-stains on it.

Without stopping to think, Hutin, as he vigorously soaped his shirt, said:

"Hallo, has there been fighting here already? Somebody wounded?"

I saw the girl blush to the tips of her ears, and the other two look sideways at her and smile.

"No," I said, "it's our Allies, our excellent Allies!"

Hutin lifted his head and looked round at me:

"Our Allies? . . ."

Then he suddenly grasped the situation.

"Good Lord, yes, of course, of course! The English! I ought to have guessed! . . ."

The morning went by quietly. We ate, smoked, wrote letters. At about noon the short, sharp, rhythmical bark of seventy-fives in action came from the neighbouring hills, and at one o'clock we received orders to go to the support of a group of artillery engaged on the heights to the north of Landres.

We had hardly moved into position when an aeroplane came over. Needless to say it was a German aeroplane. We never see any others. And a minute later shells began falling round us. Once more, as though by a miracle, the battery remained intact in the midst of the inferno of shrapnel and high explosive. But that can't last.

Ah, if I escape the hecatomb, I shall know how to live! I never realised there was a special joy in breathing, in opening one's eyes to the light, in letting oneself be penetrated by it, in being hot, in being cold, even in suffering. I thought that only certain hours were of value: the others I let go by. If I see the end of this war I shall know how to arrest them all as they pass, how to feel every second of life, like a delicious cool stream that one feels running between one's fingers. I shall always be stopping in the middle of a phrase or a gesture, simply to cry out in my heart, "I'm alive, alive!"

But quite soon, perhaps, I shall be a shapeless mass of bleeding flesh on the edge of a shell-hole. . . .

Nothing for us to do under the bombardment. The captain swept the plain through his glasses with exasperating calmness.

In the end the enemy lengthened his range, so that the shells fell behind us into a ravine with a road running through it, down which we saw a supply column gallop into safety.

Orders arrived. . . . Our batteries returned to Landres. On the way, where a shell had made a deep crater, we passed the mangled remains of a horse: a headless, legless trunk. The head lay in the ditch, intact, gazing strangely with undimmed eyes at the body. A large piece of flesh and chestnut skin had been blown to the top of the high bank. The crater, in which a pink mass of intestines sprawled in a pool of blood that was already turning black in the sun, exhaled a horrifying stench of living flesh, digested food, and dung, that would have made one vomit in another second.

We learned later that the officer who was riding the horse had not received a scratch. . . .

I watched a regiment of chasseurs coming down the high hill that dominates Landres to the north-west.

The low sun had left the deep ravine in which we were parked in shadow, but it lit up the more magnificently by contrast, with a brilliant orange glow, the steep slope down which the blue and red squadrons rode in perfect order, their drawn sabres brightly gleaming. They passed close by us, then climbed the opposite face of the valley; the red disc of the sun hung immediately above them. They seemed to be riding straight into it. On the crest, the horsemen showed for an instant in great moving lines against the western sky.

I am at the end of my strength. I can't keep myself from falling asleep. To stay awake I feel I should have to adopt the pose of the sentries of antiquity: one finger raised, in the attitude of silence.

WEDNESDAY, *September 2nd.*

The horses were not unharnessed, and after only four hours' sleep on the bare ground, which gives little rest, we were roused and had to move again.

The road ran through a thick forest. The darkness slowly gave way to a deceptive, dim half-light, the first hints of a dull, unsunny dawn. I was dozing, in spite of the jolting of the limber, to which one becomes accustomed after a time, when a cracking of broken wood and a dull thud as of something falling suddenly woke me. I looked ahead but could see nothing. Yet I seemed to hear, as well as the crunch of the wheels and the clatter of the vehicles, a moan, a noise of sobbing. . . . Yes, there came to me, quite distinctly, a childish voice crying:

"Maman! Maman!"

I just made out, by a heap of stones at the side of the road, the wheel of an overturned cart, a human form on the ground, and round it the silhouettes of children kneeling.

Sobs. The little voice again cried:

"Maman, maman! . . . Answer, maman!"

The column rolled on. A piercing, heart-rending sob, wrung from a throat choked with misery, came to my ears, seemed to penetrate my breast.

"Maman!"

One wanted to stop, to find out what it was, to do something for them. There were several children, that was certain. The mother might only have fainted. Was there a man with them? I would have jumped down off the limber and run back to them, but I knew that I should never be able to catch up the column again. Then I saw a horseman halt and dismount. He shouted:

"I'm going to stop the M.O. as he comes by. . . . I'll catch up later."

The slow march of the column bore us away. But the

horror of what had happened there, over the side of the road, kept me awake in spite of my weariness as the day slowly dawned. I felt that I should always hear that small voice crying, "Maman!" and the sobbing of those children in the grey dawn.

We came soon afterwards to the main road, where we had to halt while the infantry of the 7th Division went by. The whole Army Corps was in full retreat, and we heard that we were going to entrain.

To entrain? For what destination? What to do? It was declared that we had been relieved on the Meuse by fresh troops and that the 4th Corps was going to be reorganised. What would that mean?

Might it mean that we were going to rest? . . . If only it meant a chance to sleep! But the same thing had so often been said before in the course of the last week. Impossible to believe it now. And yet it must be true—otherwise we should be leaving all this part of the country defenceless.

All down the road, wave upon wave, with a great noise as of opened sluices, battalion after battalion marched by. The soldiers seemed fresh ; some were even singing.

The 101st Infantry Regiment came abreast of us.

"Is the 102nd behind you?" asked Tuvache.

"Yes."

"Because my brother's in it."

The stream of men flowed on and on. There at last came Tuvache's brother.

"Tuvache!"

A man turned in our direction.

"You, by God!"

The two brothers merely shook hands, but the look in their eyes showed how glad they were to see each other.

"So you're all right, eh?"

"I am. And you?"

"Me too, as you see."

"Good!"

"Heard anything from home?"

"Yes, I had a letter yesterday. They sent their love to you, and said we were to share the money they enclosed."

The infantryman searched in his pockets.

"The trouble is I haven't seen the quartermaster yet, to get the order cashed. But I can hand it over to you, if you like."

"Keep it. I've still got more left than I need."

"Good. Oh, and uncle and aunt sent their love too. Well . . . I mustn't lose my company. I hear we're going to get a rest. . . ."

"They say we are. If so, we'll be seeing each other again. . . . Au revoir!"

Their hands met. The infantryman took one step with his brother's hand still in his:

"I'll write and tell the old people I've seen you."

"Yes; I'll do the same."

The man ran off, shouldering his way through the human torrent. One saw his hand raised above the heads in the distance, waving good-bye.

We ourselves filed into the road in rear of the line regiments of the 7th Division, and an exasperatingly slow march ensued. It was very hot. The dust raised by the infantry enveloped and half choked us. We passed many dead horses lying by the side of the road.

At last, at Chatel, the battery turned aside to the left along a free road, and was able to break into a trot. Right across the hills and valleys of the landscape, as far as the horizon, a line of dust, blurring the greenery, marked the main road along which the divisions were marching.

At twelve o'clock, when I was thinking that we must have come twelve or fifteen miles since daybreak, we

German infantry advancing through Amiens,
August 1914.

suddenly heard a triple report of guns quite near at hand to the north-west.

Our leading vehicles had just emerged from the forest of Argonne and were approaching the village of Apremont. . . . Three shells burst over the village.

What could be the meaning of that? . . . Was the enemy at our heels? Were no troops holding him back? Hadn't we been relieved after all? This was defeat, then . . . invasion. . . . France at the mercy of the Germans. . . .

Carts and waggons of every description were moving along the road abreast of our column. The whole population was flying from the enemy: old women, young women, mothers with babies at their breasts, swarms of children. The poor creatures were saving their dearest possessions, their existence; the women and girls their honour, a little money, often a favourite animal: a dog, a cat, a bird in a cage.

The poorest were on foot. One family turned off down a path through a wood. There were four of them: in front was an old man with a drawn, tragic mask, carrying a large basket on a stick over his shoulder, covered with a white cloth. A sort of haversack or keeper's bag, stuffed full to bursting, knocked against his side. A young woman followed him along the narrow pathway. She was leading a fat red cow with one hand, and with the other, by means of a handkerchief knotted to its collar, a shaggy dog. A little girl hung on to her skirt and was being pulled along. An old, old woman followed behind, bent double, leaning heavily on a stick, with a grape-basket full of clothing and woollen stuff on her back.

Where were all these unfortunates going? Many of them had no idea, they told us, except that they were going straight on, into France, to wherever the Germans were not going.

"What's the good of staying?" an old man said to us.

"They burn everything just the same. We're ruined, we haven't got a home; but there it is, at least we're free. And then, you see, I've got my daughter-in-law with me, the wife of my son who's a gunner like you. She's going to have a child; she's in her seventh month. When we first heard the guns, yesterday, the pains came on. I thought the child was going to be born. That passed off. But I told her, 'We must leave at once. There's no help for it.' With swine like them, that violate and rip up women, they probably wouldn't have respected her condition. . . . We found a roadmender's hut for her to sleep in last night; God only knows what we'll do to-night. . . . I'm afraid for her health. She's sleeping in the cart just now. I've got to keep her well, somehow . . . you see, I'm responsible for her to my son. . . ."

I asked the old man, pointing ahead in the direction in which we were moving:

"What lies over there?"

"Over there?" he answered, a sudden grim look coming to his face. "What lies over there? Why, Chalons, Paris. . . . All France lies over there."

And he added, sorrowfully shaking his head:

"Ah! Nom de Dieu!"

"They're half as strong again as we are, mon pauvre bonhomme!"

He didn't answer at first. But, after a moment, he muttered:

"I saw 1870. . . . It's 1870 over again!"

The battery rolled steadily on. We had come the whole way across the Argonne. At Servons, a village on the edge of the woods, where the infantry made a long halt, we stopped for a few minutes. It was then two o'clock.

We took the horses down to the green waters of the Aisne, near a mill. They went in up to their breasts, gratefully cleansing themselves, and splashing the men who, with their knees drawn up, were also cheered by the cool freshness of the water.

Finally, near Ville-sur-Tourbe, we parked. Word went round that we were to entrain at the station, which was close by, during the evening.

I was still a prey to the hideous anxiety which had descended on me in the morning when I saw that the enemy were close behind us. What? (I thought) were we going to entrain, leaving the way clear to the invader? Wouldn't he be able, in that case, to surround and cut off the troops which were operating in Belgium and the army which had invaded Alsace? . . . But were the French still *in* Belgium and Alsace? . . . What would I not have given to know the truth, whatever it might be!

The men were in an ugly mood. No one wanted to go on the necessary fatigues. Déprez encountered the same unwillingness and inertia on all sides.

"Tuvache, water!"

"I was on water-fatigue only yesterday. . . . It's more than a mile off. . . . Some men are always on fatigue, apparently!"

"Laillé, were you on water-fatigue yesterday?"

"No. . . ."

"Then off you go!"

"Oh, hell . . . but look here . . ."

"I don't want any arguing now!"

"Some men never do a thing. . . ."

"Go and get the water, I tell you!"

"Well, at least you won't put me on to any other job afterwards?"

"All right, no."

Laillé went off very slowly, shrugging his shoulders, with a canvas bucket in each hand.

After all we found we were not to entrain at Ville-sur-Tourbe.

With only just time to swallow the soup boiling and the meat uncooked, we started off again in the red glow of twilight. The refugees were encamped for the night in the fields along the side of the road.

They had lit bivouac fires, soldier-fashion. The women and children lay in straw spread under the carts, which offered but a poor protection from the dew and the early morning chill. One saw tiny, unweaned babies sleeping in portable cradles.

We marched due south. The moon rose, and a large star glittered directly in front of us, in the axis of the road. We came to a dim town that might have been a city of the dead: Saint-Menehould. It was too dark to read the names on the signposts. The paving was uneven, the limbers jumped and jolted, the horses stumbled, the moon shone down long perspectives of empty streets. A red railway light appeared at the end of the avenue along which we were moving. Were we going to entrain? . . . No. We passed on and through the town without a halt.

Once more, in the yellow, melancholy, distance-enlarging moonlight, the open rolling country extended into infinity around us, utterly deserted, without a sign of moving troops, without a single sentry on the watch.

THURSDAY, *September 3rd.*

We halted about midnight. Orders arrived shortly afterwards, according to which we were to have moved at dawn; but these were later cancelled. Eventually we stayed here, and were able to sleep till past nine o'clock.

Now in the afternoon the stream of emigration is flowing along the road in a permanent cloud of dust.

There is a strong rumour here, in the first place that we

have definitely been relieved on the Meuse by the 6th Corps, and in the second place that we are going to Haute-Alsace to fight under the orders of General d'Amade. At the mention of this very popular name one hears men say:

"Ah, now things'll be different!"

I asked a chasseur, one of General Boëlle's orderlies, but he either knew nothing or, if he did know, wouldn't say. . . .

The carts and waggons of the refugees have had to be turned off the road into the fields to make way for the infantry of the 2nd Corps, coming from Clermont-en-Argonne and Saint-Menehould. They seem less used up than the line regiments of the 4th Corps, but they know no more about their destination than we do of ours. They, too, talk of d'Amade, victories in Alsace and in the North, and naval victories. They don't seem to think the enemy is advancing close behind us. . . . Perhaps it isn't so. Perhaps, after all, this is merely a redistribution of the French forces. Ah, if only I could believe that!

FRIDAY, *September 4th.*

We broke up our camp in the night. We should have been in good condition after a day with nothing to do but eat and sleep, had we not all been weakened by diarrhœa. Nothing could be more lowering. The doctor has no more bismuth or paregoric left, and we are reduced to chewing the bark of sloe-trees.

The horses are even more worn than the men. Many of them were slightly wounded in the fighting on Monday and Tuesday, and their wounds are festering. No veterinary aid is available; neglect, however, is not the worst of their troubles, for several of the poor brutes have had to submit to the stupid remedies devised by their drivers. One man makes a practice of urinating over his horse's pastern, which has been cut open by a shell-splinter. Almost all the horses are lame, as a result of being too tightly picketed or getting kicked during nights when the men detailed for stable-guard were too tired to keep awake.

Rarely taken out of the traces, and hardly ever unharnessed, where they are rubbed they have developed open sores on which large and small flies settle in swarms all day long. And they, too, poor wretches, like the men, are still further weakened by diarrhœa.

We continued the march all morning, passing through Givry-en-Argonne, Sommeilles, Nettancourt, Brabant. The name on the milestones changed from "Meuse" to "Marne." Dust obscured the gentle undulations of the increasingly beautiful landscape and the rich mass of the forest of Argonne to the east.

About midday we came to Revigny-aux-Vaux, a pretty, white town among meadows, and formed our park near the station by the river Ornain. While we were taking the horses to water, a man in labourer's clothes, sitting on the bank at the side of the road, hailed me.

"Where are you from, gunners?"

"From the Haute-de-Meuse, near Dun and Stenay. We've been relieved there by fresh troops."

"Relieved?"

"Yes, by the 6th Corps."

"Expect me to believe that? . . . If you said you'd run like rabbits it'd be more like the truth. . . . D'you know where the Prussians are?" he went on, standing up.

A shudder ran through me. Misery was written on the bony, ravaged features of the man, who when he had been sitting down had not seemed so tall or emaciated. His long, outstretched arm, with the hand at the end of it shaking, pointed to the north-west.

"They're at Châlons, the Prussians are, in the camp!"

I shrugged my shoulders.

"You don't believe me, eh? Well, I've just come from Châlons; an aeroplane dropped a bomb on the station as my train started. And they're at some other places too, the Prussians are, if you want to know: they're at Compiègne! D'you hear? . . . Compiègne; yes. Ask anyone round here, they'll all tell you what I'm telling you. They're at Compiègne, and took La Fère on the way."

I began trembling. Everything revolved in front of my eyes, and I felt I was going to fall. My knees instinctively tightened their grip on my horse, which slowly moved on, and brought me back to the park, haggard and as though drunk.

Hutin was there. I looked him in the eyes and slowly said:

"Hutin! The Germans are at Compiègne!"

"Where?"

"Compiègne!"

He turned pale.

"No!"

"At Compiègne!"

"Compiègne, Compiègne? Why, good God, that's only forty miles from Paris! . . ."

We looked at each other.

"Who's let them through?"

"It's the Army of the North."

"This is worse than 1870!"

"Compiègne!" repeated Hutin, horrified.

The sinister thought of the debacle, of betrayal and all the rancours of defeat, of sufferings endured in vain, rose like a black tide in every brain.

"It's what I've said all along: we've been sold," declared the trumpeter.

In spite of everything I refused to believe in betrayal.

"Sold! Why sold? Who by? . . . Who by?"

"How do I know? . . . But they wouldn't be at Compiègne if we hadn't been sold; some swine has done it! It's the same as it always was! It's '70 over again. . . . Bazaine in '70! . . ."

"No, we've simply been driven back. . . . There are so many of them! . . . They've got three times our numbers! And besides, in '70 the mistake the Army of Châlons made was in not waiting for the Germans behind Paris. That's well known. If MacMahon's Army hadn't gone forward, if it hadn't let itself get bottled up in Sedan, we might never have been beaten. . . ."

I clung to the idea of a strategic retreat. I tried to convince my comrades in order to convince myself. But they were not to be persuaded, and simply reiterated:

"It's '70 over again!"

What a ghastly refrain!

Only Bréjard, who stood listening and quietly smoking, retained his confidence.

"What certainly is damnable," he said, "is that we don't know anything. But if the other armies are like ours, there's nothing to be hopeless about. They've had a baddish knock somewhere or other, the people in the North, like us in Belgium. But as long as they haven't been captured, that's the main thing; and as for saying it's like '70 over again, it isn't in the least. In 1870 we were alone. Now, we've got the English and the Russians with us."

"Oh, don't talk to me about the English and the Russians!" interrupted Pelletier.

"Have you seen any English, sergeant?"

"No, but they're over here."

"We've been told so," corrected Millon. "And we were told we were advancing in the North. Bloody fine advance! . . ."

"And the Russians," Pelletier continued. "What's

there been to prevent them getting to Berlin, I'd like to know? They've nothing against them at all. . . ."

Bréjard shrugged his shoulders:

"They can hardly get there by train, I suppose."

"They've had a month now, though, they and their famous Cossacks!"

And the trumpeter pursued his theme:

"It's simply a pack of lies. Shall I tell you what I think, sergeant? All right then. This business of the Russians and the English declaring war against Germany's nothing but a sham . . . a sham. They've all agreed together to do us in . . . just the same as in '70."

"Yes, just the same as in '70," repeated Blanchet, who was sitting cross-legged on the ground mending a tear in his greatcoat.

We had begun to doubt everything in the blank horror of the disaster.

Why, instead of deluding us with imaginary victories, could they not have simply said to us:

"We have to do with an enemy whose numbers are greater than our own. We are consequently obliged to fall back until such time as our concentration is complete and the English reinforcements arrive"?

Were they afraid of frightening us with the word "retreat" when we had already experienced the reality?

Why? Why should they deceive us, demoralise us? . . .

Déprez, Lebidois and I went to have lunch in the garden of a restaurant, in a leafy arbour of ivy-grapes and honeysuckle, where we were surrounded with a dazzling medley of officers' uniforms: cavalry officers, infantry officers, surgeons, medical officers, officers of the intendance, pay corps officers dressed in green like foresters. . . .

We had none of us eaten off plates or drunk out of a glass for a fortnight. The meal would have been an extraordinary and delicious experience but for the thoughts of disaster which weighed on our minds.

At nightfall we entrained. The long, straw-littered platform was lit from end to end with petrol lamps. The horses, with drooping heads, stupid with exhaustion, let themselves be herded into the vans without a struggle. The guns and limbers were man-handled on to the trucks. Then in a few minutes all was still and quiet. The men settled down for the night, thirty to a van, some lying on benches, others on the floor. Folded cloaks and greatcoats served as pillows; arms and equipment were thrown into a corner. And, as the last gleam died away in the west, the train slowly slid past the dreary, deserted platform and out into the night.

SATURDAY, *September 5th.*

I had no sleep all night through. The train stopped every quarter of an hour, and men tortured with dysentery climbed over my body in their haste to jump out on to the line. The same thing is happening this morning. Whenever we come to a standstill, you see along the side of the embankment a scattered line of gunners who, when the whistle blows, hurry back to their vans pulling up their trousers as they run. Fortunately the train always moves off slowly.

A sad day, spent absently watching the country go by, one's mind hypnotised with the thought of defeat. Half the time the train goes no faster than a man could walk.

PART IV

FROM THE MARNE TO THE AISNE

SUNDAY, *September 6th.*

WAKING up to a morning of fine light and silvery mists, we found ourselves on the outskirts of Paris.

Past the forest of Fontainebleau, where troops were encamped under shelter of broom and bracken, everywhere, through the greenery, gleamed the white façades and red roofs of suburban villas. Flowers shone in the gardens. Great sunflowers turned their golden faces towards us. It was almost possible to forget the tragic reality of the hour.

Sunday. . . . There were bells ringing. And Paris was close by. The magnetic spell of the city at once began to make its influence felt. The Parisians in our waggon were beside themselves with excitement.

Very quickly after our depressing journey, and why and how it would be hard to say, fresh confidence was born in us, in spite of the news which reached us en route that the Germans had advanced beyond Creil without resistance.

It was not the strength of the entrenched camp of Paris, with its garrison of men and guns, that gave us courage; it was rather the instinctive confidence of a child which, finding itself at home again, feels invincible because of the apparent alliance of familiar things, and even of the elements. What heartened us was the inexpressible but definite sensation of a loved, formidable, immortal presence. It was like a living breath, the support of a living personality, or rather an invincible divinity; it was something quite beyond definition.

In fact, as Hutin repeated:

"It's Paris! That's what it is—Paris!"

"The English!"

A trainload of British troops went by us, with much shouting and waving of caps on both sides.

The station at Villeneuve-Saint-Georges was full of Highlanders. Our train stopped. The Scotchmen examined our guns with curiosity. Lebidois served as interpreter. There was much shaking of hands and more shouting.

Little Millon accosted a brawny Highlander with tattooed wrists and knees. He wanted to know whether he wore any garment under his kilt. The other was puzzled, not understanding, and laughed.

"My boy," declared Millon, "with a bit more hair hanging down your back and a bit less on your legs, you'd pass anywhere for a flapper in that little short petticoat of yours."

We detrained at Pantin. Except for the inscriptions on the wooden panels or iron blinds of the shops—"*Le patron est à la guerre*," or, in letters a foot high, "*Maison française*"—and the mobilisation notices, with their flags already stained and faded, Pantin wore its usual summer Sunday aspect.

Footpath and roadway were thronged with a moving crowd of women in light dresses, neatly corsetted and smart as only Parisiennes know how to make themselves, and soldiers of all arms, sauntering idly along as though out for an ordinary morning stroll. A Territorial went by with his wife on his arm and a little boy holding on to his other hand.

Could the enemy really be at the gates, one wondered?

We have moved into billets at Rosny-sous-Bois, on a height dominating the city in one direction, and in the other the barren-looking, unattractive plain of Brie. From the distance, towards the south-east, comes the rumble of gun-fire.

In the streets, between the greenery of gardens and the light façades of the villas, the red uniforms, the women's white blouses and their gay moving sunshades, make brilliant splashes of colour in the crowd.

The zouaves have come in from the fortifications.

Outside the cafés, where not a seat is to be had, the white aprons of the waiters flit in and out among the many-coloured costumes of chasseurs, supply corps men, artillerymen, tirailleurs and spahis. There are queues in front of the post-office, and at the doors of the bakers' and confectioners' shops. Women run here and there, accosting soldiers, asking for news, looking for husbands, sons, brothers or lovers who may have arrived in the town.

The movement is perpetual, with much jostling, hailing of friends, drinking, eating, smoking and laughter. Families of bourgeois, placid and curious, forge through the human torrent with their little stubborn steps.

And all the time the guns are rumbling in the distance. But, to hear them, you must go a little apart from the crowd, down the lanes between the gardens.

It seems there has been fighting to-day on the Grand-Morin.

MONDAY, *September 7th.*

It was broad daylight when Bréjard shouted:

"Up with you!"

"What is it?"

"Listen here."

He drew a paper from his pocket.

"ARMY ORDER OF THE DAY

"*On the eve of a battle on which the country's safety depends, all ranks are reminded that there is to be no more looking to the rear: every effort must be directed towards attacking the enemy and driving him back. Troops which can advance no farther must at all costs hold their ground and resolve to die rather than retire.*"

"D'you hear that?"

Yes, we heard. We should never have been able to express our own innermost thoughts so simply and completely.

"'Troops must resolve to die rather than retire.' That's that, then."

"And now, fall in!" added Bréjard. "We're for it!"

Two girls, the sister and fiancée of one of my comrades, came up as the battery moved off. For a moment they ran alongside the horses, flushed and panting. They spoke very rapidly, both together. When they felt their breath failing, they held a hand out, one after the other, to the gunner, who leaned down across the neck of his horse to kiss their fingers.

Leaving the outskirts of the town, we took the main Soissons road, and were soon moving across the level plain of Brie. Towards the sound of the guns. We clearly felt that we were living through the heaviest, most portentous hours of a century, perhaps of a nation's history.

We might have been depressed by the dreariness of the landscape, which had nothing to break its monotony but an occasional empty trench, littered with straw, and the lean poplars, in lines or clumps, had we not all the time felt Paris behind us, and the pulsing life of Paris.

Said Hutin to me:

"If we've got to go west somewhere, I'd sooner it was here than away on the Meuse."

"Why?"

"Damned if I know!"

Evening found us, after ten hours on the road, still moving. Far in the distance to our rear, the dark silhouette of Montmartre stood out against the western sky.

All the landscape was bathed in the light of the stars, which shone this evening with great brilliance. Only the road, beneath its vault of tall trees that met overhead, was absolutely dark. A distant searchlight swept the plain. The battery advanced at the trot. It was a pavé road, and the vehicles shook and jolted till we who sat on the limbers were doubled up with intolerable pain. It became difficult to breathe; with bursting chests, thumping hearts and buzzing ears, feeling sick and giddy, we literally sweated with agony. Were we ever to stop, we wondered?

Hour after hour we followed the same dark road. The column slowed down to a walk. An enormous headlight, swiftly approaching, opened up dizzy cathedral perspectives under the trees, and made strange shifting shadows of each team and rider as they emerged from the pitch night. The car shot past us.

On, on we rolled. . . . Were we never going to stop?

"Halt!"

At last! We parked in a field. The horses had still to be watered.

In an obscure village an acetylene lamp, shedding a glow on great copper pans in a kitchen, was the only light.

There was no drinking-place. We had to push on and pick our way across meadows, mostly morass, to the nearest stream. The banks were too high for the horses to reach the running water, and we had to give it them in the canvas buckets.

On our way back to the village, a torrent of horses filled the roadway. More batteries had arrived.

A block had brought me momentarily to a halt against the boundary-wall of a château, when a car, with all its lights extinguished, ploughing its way through the throng, forced a confused wave of men and beasts against me, the weight of which flattened me against the wall. . . . Another car followed in its wake, then others and still others, hundreds of them, in endless, silent succession.

The moon had risen, and its rays shone reflected on the shiny peaks of taxi-drivers' caps. Inside the cabs one could make out the bent heads of sleeping soldiers.

Someone asked:

"Wounded?"

And a passing voice replied:

"No. The 7th Division. From Paris. Going into the line! . . ."

Tuesday, *September 8th.*

"Stand to!"

Pitch darkness. The embers still glowed in the grates. The noise of gun-fire was continuous. The great flashes of each discharge pierced the night like summer lightning. Not far off, to the west, a farm was blazing, or perhaps some haystacks. It was warm. A floating odour of corruption filled the air.

The battery formed up in the roadway and moved off.

At Dammartin, through which we passed as day broke, there were German inscriptions, billeting numbers, chalked on the closed doors and shutters. On the door of a barn I read these words, written in pointed gothic letters: "Gute Leute" (good people). Who lived there? I asked myself.

As we emerged from the village, the deep roar of the guns seemed to come from the bowels of the earth. It was unintermittent now.

A tomb by the roadside: a wooden cross, with a name written on it in tar, surmounted by a chasseur's helmet with its brass chin-strap. The man had not been buried deep enough, and a pungent smell rose from the loose, sun-cracked soil.

Dead horses lay at frequent intervals along the road, blown out like leather bottles, their stiff legs and bright, iron-shod hoofs pointing to the sky. From a wound in the flank of a great chestnut mare the worms had spread on to the grass. They swarmed in the anus, and fell to the ground in a putrid watery mass. They came out of the nostrils and mouth, and out of a hole made by a revolver bullet near the ear.

"At a trot—march!"

The battery disappeared in the cloud of its own dust. We began to pass wounded men, hundreds of them, infantry of the line, chasseurs and marines, white with dust, and with bloodstained bandages. They were helping one another along, and for the most part moved in little groups. Many stopped by the roadside. It was growing hot. I saw several of them round an apple tree, shaking the fruit down. They were thirsty, and the apples refreshed them.

We halted while a staff officer gave orders to our major. I spoke to a marine with a wound in his head.

"What's it like up in front?"

"They're falling thick!"

It was not clear whether he meant bullets and shells or men. But one could easily tell, by the expression on the taut, haggard features, that the struggle was fierce.

"Has the fighting been going on long?"

"Yes."

"How many days?"

"It began before we arrived."

"When did you arrive?"

"Day before yesterday."

And he said again:

"They're falling thick."

We moved on again, still at the trot.

The blue sky, very clear and pure on the northern and western horizon, was dappled with white puffs of bursting shrapnel. In the distance were the black bursts of incendiary and high-explosive shells.

The odour of corruption pursued us; it unsettled us, became an obsession, made us look everywhere for corpses.

One of the horses belonging to my limber suddenly refused to go any farther, and brought the whole team to a stop. It was dead lame, and had to be turned loose and abandoned. The rest of the battery, meanwhile, went ahead. With the remaining five horses we galloped across fields to rejoin the column, the furrows shaking us so that we had to cling to our places with tooth and nail to avoid falling off.

We caught up with the battery half-way through a village which had been visible from far off across the bare countryside. The enemy had been there; the doors had been battered in with rifle-butts. The panes were broken in almost all the windows, which were mere frames lined with spikes of broken glass. The soiled curtains floated through them dismally from inside. Shutters torn from their hinges lay on the sidewalk among broken bottles and a litter of pots and pans. Others, hanging by one hinge, flapped against the walls.

Through the wide-open doors one could see shattered chests and cupboards, overturned in the middle of the rooms. Empty drawers, mantelpiece ornaments, portraits and engravings lay in confusion on the raddled floors. Linen clothing and mud-stained sheets, still bearing the impression of heavy nailed boots, were strewn even in the middle of the street, and gave the unhappy houses something of the horror of disembowelled bodies.

The roadway was littered with chairs and tables thrown from the windows, perambulators, broken casks. Wood cracked under our wheels as we went. There was a pair of pink stays floating in the stream.

On a Michelin signpost at the end of a village I read: "Drive slowly: children," and the inscription on the reverse, "Thank you," was lamentable and a mockery.

We halted on a road that made a great white line across a plain of growing beetroot. A barn, three haystacks, and farther off some geometrical clumps of trees and a long line of poplars, were all that broke the dreary monotony of the level fields. To the north and east the battle rumbled, hissed and crashed like a storm at sea. It might have been the noise of some appalling world cataclysm.

We stayed where we were, waiting. And suddenly the landscape became populous. Battalions, debouching from Sennevières, deployed into open formation, and other men, hundreds, thousands whose presence had till then been unsuspected, got up from the ground and surged forward. Their red trousers, as far as the eye could see, showed against the sombre green of the fields. Frightened hares fled before the advancing lines.

Wounded began to appear again, coming back in little groups. We could see them far away, dark spots on the luminous surface of the sun-baked road.

Somewhere near by a regiment of cuirassiers was billeted. A number of them came past us on foot, without helmets or cuirasses, wearing only their felt under-jerkins with thickly padded sleeves. They were carrying great quarters of fresh meat. Over to the right, on the edge of the village, in the shade of three poplars, close to a dead horse, some men were slaughtering bullocks and selling the flesh.

The order came at last:

"Reconnaissance!"

I found that I was still unable to suppress the little shiver of apprehension which this order has invariably produced in me so far.

When we reached our battery position, we found the only cover consisted of a hedge of briars and straggling bushes. There could be no doubt the battery was visible to the enemy from several points on the horizon. The place could hardly have been worse; but none better offered in the immediate neighbourhood.

Our officers had established the command-post on a cart-track near No. 1 gun. In front, the whole battlefield lay open before us. But in all the landscape, which, being almost without hill or valley, seemed incapable of mystery, and where yet we knew that the fate of France was at stake, not a man or gun was to be seen. The thundering desert seemed motionless beneath the bursting shells. . . .

All at once we fell asleep in the sunshine, with the unconsciousness of pawns that are moved on a chess-board, and with a fatalism that was the inevitable result of the precarious existence we had led during the past month.

A word of command woke me. The sun was low in the west behind us.

"Take post!"

Something dark, that might have been artillery, was moving over there, at the foot of some wooded hills, more than five thousand yards away. We opened fire. To the right and left, and even in front of us, batteries of seventy-fives, one after the other, came into action. Whenever our own guns were silent for a few seconds we heard their rapid drum-fire all round us.

Out in front all was still. The captain gave the order to cease fire. But the smoke from the powder, and the dust raised from the dry soil by the shock of our firing, had scarcely drifted away, when three big shells burst along the hedge that masked our position, making three wide gaps in it. The smoke of their explosion shut off all the eastern horizon from our view.

"They've seen our flashes," said Bréjard.

"Nothing much wrong with their aim, either," added Hutin. "Five-nines!"

As ill-luck would have it, an ammunition-waggon chose this precise moment to come up at a trot, under a corporal mounted on a big white mare.

Loud shouts greeted him.

"Dismount!"

"Dis-*mount!* D'you want to get us all killed?"

The driver seemed not to hear.

"Dismount, blast you! Walk! . . . Walk!!"

But already they had unhooked the full waggon and hooked in the empty one, and off they went at a gallop, despite our shouts.

The enemy did not keep us waiting long. We soon heard the whistle of another salvo on its way to us. The sound was curiously modulated by the wind. We listened to it for seconds on end. . . .

The great, invisible deaths, falling slowly from the sky, were an interminable torture. Everything vibrated. . . . Then the shells burst; the wind swept the smoke of the explosion on to us.

I heard a rattling cry.

"Ooh . . . ooh . . . ooh . . . ooh . . . ooh."

Our own battery was untouched; the ammunition-waggon was still in sight, making off at full speed; and a gunner belonging to the battery next to us was in the throes of death. Blood from the hole in his forehead was dripping over the empty shell-cases that lay on the ground beside him.

Hutin, still seated in his firing position, suddenly shouted:

"I can see the b—s shooting! I can see them . . . over there . . . a good nine thousand metres away. I saw the flash. . . . There's another—look out, it's coming!"

A moment later came the shock of another salvo. I instinctively shut my eyes, and felt a shower of dirt spatter on my face. I was unhurt; a large fragment went droning slowly into the distance. Once more the battery was enveloped in smoke. I heard the clear tones of the captain's voice shouting to the sergeant-major:

"Daumain, get the men under cover to the right. C.O.'s order. No good getting killed while we're not firing."

The order was shouted along, and we emerged from the smoke and got out of the line of the enemy's fire. But it seemed to pursue us as we scattered and ran across the field with hunched-up shoulders.

A shell burst close by me with a blinding flash, and knocked over the sergeant of No. 12 battery. He got up again immediately. There were two atrociously symmetrical red gashes over his eyes. He went on, holding his head up to prevent the blood running into his eyes. I wanted to help him, but he said:

"I'm all right. . . . You run along. It's nothing. . . . There's life in the old horse yet! . . ."

We collected behind two big haystacks, and while we pulled ourselves together and waited for further orders, we took stock of the situation.

"11th Battery?"

"11th."

"Hutin?"

"Here!"

"Not hit?"

"No. You all right?"

"Perfectly."

The four gun detachments were present in full.

"What about the captain?"

"He's still out at the observation-post. Look. . . . You can see his elbow sticking out beyond that tree. He's all right."

Two more salvos burst near our guns, which still seemed intact.

How long the night was in coming! That great red sun, so near the horizon now, would it never disappear behind the beetroot-field? . . . It might have been fixed in its course, motionless for ever.

Hutin hurled an oath at its glowing face.

Out in front, the captain signalled to us with a sweep of his arm.

A shout went up among us behind the haystacks.

"Take post!"

We were going to begin firing again. But no. New orders had come.

"Limber up!"

A fog, rising from the valleys of the plain, had masked its features. The distant hills whence the shelling had come were hidden in a purplish mist. But surely we must be visible from there, silhouetted against the clear eastern sky?

The limbers came up, and we hooked in and moved away. There was no more shelling.

By now the rifle and machine-gun fire in front had died down. The guns, too, left off firing. An extraordinary silence descended on the landscape. Conflagrations, increasingly conspicuous as the night grew darker, blazed at different points on the plain.

The fierce struggle of the day had resulted in no decision. The adversaries rested in their respective positions.

WEDNESDAY, *September 9th.*

We were making coffee in a field near Sennevières, under orders to be ready to move at a moment's notice. It was hot. The lull in the fighting had continued until well after dawn, but later, to the east and north-east, the cannonade became as continuous as yesterday.

Quite suddenly, at about midday, the line of firing to our left bent back and extended outwards. We were on the extreme left wing of the French Armies. And we were filled with apprehension. Was the enemy working round our flank?

We questioned the captain, who, like ourselves, was looking towards some woods which, yesterday, had been outside the field of action, but which were now being heavily bombarded by the enemy.

"What's happening, sir?"

"I know no more about it than you, my friends. I merely obey orders. I go or stay wherever I'm told to go or stay. That's all there is to it."

Déprez insisted:

"But they're turning our flank again."

The captain's fine features betrayed his anxiety.

"Yes," he said, "they're shelling some woods that they weren't shelling yesterday. Which at least proves they haven't advanced that far. They may even be threatened by an enveloping movement of our own troops from that direction. . . . Who knows? . . . Besides, if they are in fact outflanking us, we're not alone here. We'll hold our ground."

He searched our faces with his proud, intelligent, grey-blue eyes, and repeated:

"We'll hold our ground, eh?"

"We will, sir."

When the coffee was hot, the captain pulled his aluminium cup from his pocket and dipped it into the pot of steaming liquid. All the men of the team stood waiting beside him, mug in hand. When the captain had filled his cup, each bent down in turn to take his share. Silently we savoured the coffee.

Then the cook declared:

"There's another go still!"

"How much have you?" asked the captain, careful to see that the distribution should be equal.

"A good quarter-pint all round."

The captain had his, then the men. And, as there was still some coffee left, mingled with the grounds, the operation was repeated a third time.

All at once, with the horrible suddenness which we had remarked every time we had had to retire in the Meuse fighting, the countryside was peopled with lines of infantry. Companies and battalions emerged from woods and from behind hedgerows, and got up from standing corn, and massed in the valleys.

"What now?" asked Bréjard.

"Are they clearing off, the brutes?" exclaimed Millon, folding his arms.

The captain looked anxiously at the moving infantry.

"No," he said; "they're support troops, shifting to the north to make a defensive flank in case the enemy attacks in that direction."

Orders arrived: to take up a position between Sennevières and Nanteuil-le-Haudouin.

This made it still more apparent that our flank was being turned. A wave of fierce anger ran through us. Were they going to get past us, to Paris? Was there to be death and looting and violating in our own homes?

"Ah!" exclaimed Hutin, "if I could only get a sight of the ——s, to blast hell out of them!"

"Trot!" came the captain's word of command.

Leaning across their horses' collars, the drivers urged their teams forward with voice, whip, knees and spurs. A single breath seemed to sweep the whole brigade of artillery—men, beasts and guns—across the bare fields and over the undulating furrows.

We took up a position from which we could fire to the north-west. Behind us the sun, already low, lit up the railway and road between Nanteuil and Paris, along which ran a line of poplars.

More bodies of infantry began falling back. Millon raised his voice again:

"They're giving way, the useless brutes! Curse them! Haven't they read the army order?"

A minute later the fusillade broke out behind us. We were outflanked. . . .

Large bodies of infantry were debouching from Nanteuil along the main Paris road and between the road and the railway line. The enemy was enveloping us in an immense horseshoe. It looked as though the 4th Corps was left with no possible line of retreat but a narrow passage between Sennevières and Silly, to the south-west.

An officer in an airman's helmet drove up in a motor-car and ran to the observation-post.

The commanding officer issued orders for the guns to be switched completely round.

We were liable to be caught between two fires at any moment, for north-west of Nanteuil, on the high ground dominating the road, it was not to be doubted that the enemy would put guns to support the advance of his infantry.

Our batteries opened fire.

In a moment a kind of frenzy took possession of both men and guns. The guns were like roaring monsters, infuriated dragons that belched flames at the face of the sun as it slowly sank in the rich summer dusk. Piles of smoking empties accumulated behind the guns. Where our shells fell we could see men scattering, running in all directions, falling in heaps. From the heights dominating Nanteuil, from which we were undoubtedly under observation, no enemy artillery replied.

The massacre went on and on.

"Ah! *They*'ll never see Paris, that's certain!"

Night fell. The line regiments began falling back in an orderly manner along the valley above which we were stationed. A troop of chasseurs went by at a trot, followed by a whole brigade of cuirassiers. The army was in retreat. . . .

We were beaten, then . . . beaten. . . . The enemy was advancing on Paris. . . .

The sun had become a mere crescent on the horizon. The mounted troops, moving towards Silly, disappeared in the dust they raised. We still went on firing, raining shells on the plain of beetroot-fields, where figures could still be seen moving here and there.

"Cease fire!"

There were some who either did not or would not hear. . . . Three guns went on firing. The major had to repeat the order, shouting at the top of his voice.

The red and sweating men sponged themselves. Then they stood behind their guns with folded arms, and silently contemplated the dusky fields, not an inch of which had been spared.

We were waiting for our own orders to retreat.

But when the order came it was to stay where we were for the night. A battalion of infantry was sent to cover us, and deployed and took up a position two hundred yards from our park, which we formed on the spot.

It appears there are no other French troops between us and the enemy. We are at the mercy of any force of cavalry which may choose to attack us during the night.

THURSDAY, *September 10th.*

After yesterday's experience we expected a furious bombardment as soon as day broke. Instead, everything was quiet. . . . The sun's rays lit up all the plain and the rising ground where we stood, motionless and ready for action, waiting for the enemy. Not a shot was fired; which surprised us, and made us uneasy.

A colonel, coming by at the head of an infantry battalion, recognised our commanding officer and spoke to him:

"'Morning, Solente!"

"'Morning!"

"How are things with you?"

"Well enough."

"What are you doing there with your little lot?"

"Covering the Nanteuil road."

"You haven't heard, then?"

"No, what?"

"The enemy cleared off in the night."

"What's that?"

"Yes. We've got orders to move forward. . . . The Germans are retreating all along the line."

The two officers looked at each other and smiled.

"That means——"

"Yes, it's a victory."

The news, as it passed from mouth to mouth, shook us with joy. Victory, victory . . . when we were so far from expecting it!

Towards noon we had orders to advance.

At Nanteuil there were already signs of life again. A grocer was unfastening the wooden shutters of his shop. Windows opened as we went through the town. As at Dammartin, I read on several doors the inscription: "Gute Leute."

The road along which our column moved led past the fields where we had stopped the enemy's attack yesterday. We halted there, doubtless to await new orders.

The countryside was very still. But, between the main Paris road and the railway, grey-clad corpses lay among the beetroot, as far as the eye could see. At the edge of a field of standing maize six Germans sprawled in a heap. The last to die had fallen on his back on top of the others. His stiffened legs, raised on a human rump, stuck up towards the sky, and his neck was bent under the weight of his body, so that the chin touched the chest. With his wide, staring eyes, and his mouth twisted into a horrible grin, the dead Prussian, whose helmet was still on, seemed to be trying to look at his navel. Of the other corpses in the heap, all that could be seen was a confusion of shoulders, backs of necks and boot-heels. But one of them, half buried under the carcases of his comrades, had evidently not died quickly. His scalp had been torn off by a shell, which had also carried away the imperial eagle from his helmet; and the man had struggled to get free of the frightful load that pinned down his legs and the lower half of his body. The effort had been in vain. Only his breast and shoulders emerged from the heap. Raised on one elbow, with his mouth wide open, screaming, so he must have died, reaching out one great gnarled fist towards the hills we had just left, and from which death had come to him. The fleshy parts of his face, already a greenish colour, had fallen in, and one had a vision, through the mask from which all signs of life had faded, of the hollow-eyed, bare-toothed, square-chinned face of Death.

A little way off three supply corps men were bending over a Prussian who lay face upwards, with his arms crooked as though ready for some frightful embrace. As one of them raised the head of the corpse, in order to remove the helmet, a stream of dark blood suddenly gushed from the open mouth over his hands. You could see him ejaculate "Swine!" as he wiped his dirtied hands in the folds of the German's grey cloak.

A subaltern of engineers was counting the dead bodies preparatory to burying them.

"Is this some of your work, gunners? I've counted seventeen hundred already. And I'm not through yet. There must be two thousand at least."

As I moved away, feeling a little weak, through the maize, my foot caught in something. The soft impact signified a corpse, and I jumped hastily aside.

Forward, towards the north.

The road was littered with Mausers, short bayonets like butchers' knives, ammunition-pouches, helmets, cowhide packs, holsters, saddles and dead horses.

The Ruettes road, on the evening of the Battle of Virton, had been the same. Then I had thought, a little surprised, in my worn-out condition: "I'm taking part in a French defeat." And to-day I found myself equally astonished at having taken part in a victory, the proofs of which were there before me: a victory that had saved Paris, had saved France, perhaps, and might be the starting-point of a new era. Looking at that calvary of the German Army, we told ourselves that the enemy would soon be leaving France as quickly as he had entered it.

We passed a wide, level field in which there was a yellow line of newly dug earth, with rifles stuck along it butt-ends upwards, contrasting strongly with the green grass. Hundreds of men, perhaps thousands, had been buried there. All the pestilence of their decomposition escaped through the dry, cracked soil and came to our nostrils along the wind. There were other pits at intervals along the road, into which bodies had been thrown, and from each rose the same smell, catching one by the throat. I found myself uneasily sniffing the air, like a dog when it feels the presence of death.

We halted for a time near some sappers who were shovelling earth into a hole that they had just dug. A chestnut crupper was still visible, marked "Uh. 3" (3rd Uhlans).

The impression of the beast's carcase could be seen in the soft earth at the side of the pit. There were worms swarming there in a pool of congealed blood.

One of the sappers paused from shovelling, and straightened himself.

"Pah! what a stink the brute makes," he said. "It's a dirty job, this. Trust me not to be a grave-digger when the war's over. The horses are worse than the men. We'll be catching the plague before we're through with it!"

"When I tried to pull him along," declared another, "the hoof came away in my hand."

And he pointed with his foot to the iron-shod hoof, lying like a large flint on the ground.

At another place, in a newly harrowed field that had been trampled by the hoofs of two galloping horses, lay two lances, one of them broken, a light cavalry sabre, a uhlan's helmet and a water-bottle. One visualised the strange combat that had taken place there.

It began to turn misty. The landscape, monotonous and wan under the grey sky, and still strewn, though less thickly, with dead bodies, arms and equipment, filled us with a gloom that was almost physically painful. One had to say over and over again to oneself, "This is victory," to realise the deep joy that was at the bottom of our hearts, the joy of knowing that the country is saved.

SATURDAY, *September 12th.*

It has rained incessantly for two days. We have gone forward more than forty kilometres through the downpour. The enemy's retreat has been rapid, and is only feebly covered by a few batteries that seem short of ammunition. Each hour makes our victory more conclusive, and everyone would be very happy but for the rain.

The captain has sent me back to the waggon-lines for a few days, partly on account of a persistent and very weakening attack of diarrhœa, and partly on account of a bad cut in one of my wrists. This leaves me comparatively free from duties, with better cooked food to eat and plenty of time for sleep.

While our batteries were harassing the retreating German columns with a fierce bombardment, the waggon-lines installed themselves in an open ravine, in which the rain seemed to converge from every point of the horizon. Shells fell there too, but buried themselves without bursting in a near-by marsh, throwing up geysers of mud.

It was here that the sergeant of No. 6 gun, to which I am temporarily attached, called:

"Roll up, *poilus*!"

"Here we all are," answered a grey-headed old fellow, a voluntarily enlisted man. "Poilus without a dry hair between us!" [1]

"Listen to this."

And the sergeant, in a hoarse voice, proceeded to read out an order of the day:

---

[1] *Poilu*, the favourite French slang for soldier = *hairy, unshaven*.

The aftermath.

"*The Sixth Army has been hotly engaged, for five days on end, against a numerous adversary whose morale had been raised to the highest pitch by his former successes. The struggle has been fierce, the losses by fire and the strain due to lack of sleep and sometimes food, have surpassed imagination; you have borne all with a valour, firmness and endurance to which no words of mine can do justice.*

"*Comrades, the commander-in-chief asked you, in the name of our country, to do more than your duty; you answered with deeds that seemed wellnigh impossible. Thanks to you, victory has crowned our colours. Now that you have tasted its glorious satisfactions, you will not let its fruits escape you.*

"*As for me, if I have done anything towards it, I have been more than rewarded by the greatest honour which has been granted me in the course of a long career, the honour of commanding such men as you.*

"*With the deepest gratitude I thank you for what you have done, for I owe you that to which all my energy and all my efforts have been directed for forty-four years: the avenging of 1870.*

"*My thanks to you, and honour to all ranks of the Sixth Army.*

"*Signed:* JOFFRE.
"*Countersigned:* MAUNOURY."

"That's well said!" declared a voice.

"Sergeant-major," cried the old volunteer, "if the general's so pleased with us, I wish you'd ask him to have the taps turned off for a bit up in the sky."

Soon afterwards we moved again. The country through which we had been advancing since daybreak, with short halts of an hour or two while the batteries fired, seemed at first glance to be an endless flat plain, almost wholly deserted. Beetroot-fields and cornfields, in which the harvest, still for the most part in sheaves, was rapidly going to ruin, seemed to stretch in endless succession from horizon to horizon under the low, grey, mournful sky, from which the cold rain poured down remorselessly. But suddenly, in the midst of the bare landscape, an unsuspected valley would open before us, thickly wooded, and so deep that the very church tower of the village at the bottom was almost buried.

Under the downpour the teams forged ahead with heads down and ears twitching, because of the rain that tickled them. Their coats glistened. Many of our beasts were already on their last legs, and had only been kept going by a miracle. The weather finished them off. Three horses had to be abandoned one after the other in rapid succession. Having reached the extreme limit of their endurance, they suddenly stumbled and stood still in their tracks. No power on earth could have made them stir another inch, and they had to be unharnessed and left, doubtless to die where they stood.

The men were glum and silent under their dark cloaks. The rain ran down our necks and froze us. Many of the drivers reversed their caps, so that the brims kept the water off their necks. Their faces, contracted by the stinging impact of the rain, were half hidden under the high turned-up collars. The shirts stuck to our shoulders and the trousers to our knees. The soaked garments absorbed the natural heat of the body, so that we had the horrible sensation of being slowly frozen; the life seemed to be departing out of our limbs, as if we were dying by inches.

We passed wretched-looking, drenched infantrymen on the road. The water poured from the flattened folds of their capes. Many of them had covered their shoulders with sacks. One man had a woman's petticoat over his head and back; others were using bed-curtains, quilts and various articles of clothing for the same purpose.

The road was a river of liquid mud, in which neither men, beasts nor vehicles left any trace of their passage.

As evening fell the grey vault of the sky came lower still, contracting the horizon of the fields, and meeting the very earth. Mist enveloped and enshrouded us. It was impossible to tell in which direction the sun set; the west was as colourless as the east; the diffused, dirty light of day grew gradually fainter; one still made out, here and there by the roadside, the dark forms of dead horses; then it was night. The rain had run down under my clothes as far as my loins. I was as cold as ice, and felt more and more acutely the indescribable sensation of life slowly ebbing from my body. On, on we rolled through the night. . . .

It may have been ten o'clock when the column at last halted at the entrance to a village and drew in to the side of the road. But we had still a long wait there, huddled motionless on our seats, with chattering teeth, growing colder and colder. Doubtless there was some obstruction ahead, a convoy going by, or a cross-roads—something, we knew not what, that delayed our advance. . . .

It seemed as if we were fated to spend the whole night there under the rain.

But in the end we were able to move on, and turned into a field, where we parked our vehicles and picketed the horses. Yellow points from the lanterns appeared here and there, but scarcely penetrated the thick darkness. There was no sound but the splash and clatter of the feet of men and horses, heavy with exhaustion, in the liquid mud.

The battery cook shouted for the section commanders to send ration parties. But no distribution was made; the tired men went off, preferring to wait till to-morrow before touching food. The cook's voice came out of the darkness, pointing out that if there was an alarm during the night, we ran the risk of having to go through the day with empty stomachs. He was right; but no one paid any attention.

We moved in groups of two and three through the darkness, which was so dense that one had to be continually calling out in order not to lose one's way.

"11th! . . . Here you are; this way, 11th!"

Passing convoys bespattered us with mud. A wheel grazed my elbow. After what seemed an age, one found no better cover than wretched barns open to the four winds, with a few wisps of damp straw to lie on. And there, silent, soaked through, and reeking with the smell of wet animals, we turned in for a few hours of miserable, shivering, comfortless sleep, continually disturbed by the cries of men dreaming.

SUNDAY, *September 13th.*

We woke to find the sun shining. There were still low clouds in the west; but these soon dispersed, and our spirits correspondingly revived. The sky was blue from horizon to horizon when we resumed our forward march.

The enemy artillery still kept up a desultory and ineffective fire. There is no doubt the Germans are badly demoralised. We were told in the villages that we were only two hours behind the last of their stragglers. It seems that their retreat became a rout yesterday. Infantrymen without their rifles, and gunners and cavalry without horses, were seen running pell-mell, as hard as they could go, harassed by shells from our seventy-fives and pursued by our advance-guards.

At Vic-sur-Aisne, while waiting for our turn to cross the river by a pontoon bridge, I went into a pretty house which the Germans had left with all the doors and windows gaping. The cupboards and chests of drawers had all been broken in and rifled. The staircase was strewn with petticoats, chemises and women's underclothing. A meal was ready laid on the dining-room table, but the overturned chairs showed how hastily the guests had taken their departure. I was hungry, and automatically picked up a chair and sat down to table. The luncheon was excellent, though cold.

When at last the leading teams of the column moved off on to the bridge, I learned, before leaving Vic, that I had eaten the meal that had been prepared for the Grand Duke of Mecklenburg-Schwerin, but which had been interrupted by the arrival of the French advance-guards.

We crossed the Aisne without hindrance, wondering how it was that the enemy made no attempt to stop us. The thought of some hidden ambush, such as those we had laid for the Germans when they crossed the Meuse, gave me considerable anxiety.

Near Attichy, while our batteries got into position, the waggon-lines halted on a road that wound steeply upwards to the high ground through dense woods, still wet and fragrant from yesterday's rain. I lay down with two or three other men in some tall bracken, at the entrance to a sunny little quarry of white stone by the side of the road, and was on the point of going to sleep when suddenly a shell burst close by with a shattering explosion that made every leaf and twig in sight rustle and vibrate.

A man appeared round the side of the quarry, very pale and scared-looking. He was holding his right elbow in his left hand, and sank down in the bracken, murmuring:

"I'm hit."

"Where?"

With a little movement of his head he indicated his elbow, from which blood was dripping. And at the same moment from down the road, which, just beyond where we lay, made two sharp turns and disappeared under a vault of tall birch trees, came a confused noise of groans, shouts and trampling hoofs.

A driver arrived, bareheaded and with blood on his face.

"Come quickly . . . down there, that shell . . . in the middle of the road. Everything's smashed up; the horses are all over the place. . . . God!"

"You're hit."

"Where?"

"In the cheek."

"No, it's from a horse, my off-horse. . . . Come on, hurry!"

More shells went hissing by. We raced down the road. As I rounded the corner an appalling sight brought me to a sudden standstill and momentarily took every breath out of my body.

In the white roadway, mottled by the sunshine that came through the leaves of the trees overhead, lay a formless mass of sprawling men and horses. The entire teams of the forge-waggon and battery cart had been smashed into a moving pile of bleeding flesh. On top were men. Two drivers lay in the road face downwards. Others were crawling on hands and knees among the prostrate saddle-horses. Wounded men were stirring in the ditches by the side of the road.

Long-drawn-out groans, strange, plaintive noises like the piercing cries of beasts of the night, an unending, dull "ooooh! . . . ooooh!" rising and falling like the chant of some tribe of savages. Blood was running in streams along the ruts at each side of the road. A sickening slaughter-house stench, a sort of damp warmth, an odour of smoking flesh and trickling life, a smell of horses, entrails and digested food, caught me by the throat and overwhelmed me with horror, misery and disgust.

A man whose head and body down to the waist were buried under the forge-waggon team had succeeded in sticking one of his arms out through a mass of spreading horse-guts, but the entrails clung to his wrist and pinioned it. He was shaking them to and fro furiously, sending out spurts of blood. Dying horses discharged wind and dung, and scraped the ground with their stiffened legs. Their iron shoes grated on the stones. Chains and traces snapped as they writhed in their death-struggle. The waggon to which they were fastened kept shifting backwards and forwards.

A dead infantryman lay face upwards with a gaping wound in his chest. His blue, wide-open eyes had a perplexed stare in them that seemed to go right through me. A gunner had been pinned to the bank, and was stuck there, almost upright, with a great open gash in his stomach; a wounded horse lay motionless over his feet, bleeding at the nostrils.

When for a brief interval there was a pause in the noise of groans and death-rattles, one became aware of the sound of running blood, and the audible slither of the pink and whitish-grey intestines coiling and uncoiling in the roadway.

I ran to the help of the man buried under the forge-waggon team, who was suffocating. He emerged with horribly twisted features, entirely red, his hair and beard clotted with blood, and rolling the whites of his eyes like a man in a fit. Another man, wounded in the loins, was in danger of being kicked to death by a dying horse. I quickly shot the beast with my revolver. And it was only then that I caught sight of my friend M——, lying between two horses, very pale and with eyes closed. I ran to him and passed my arm under his body to raise him up, when every drop of blood suddenly seemed to dry up in my veins and my heart to stop beating. . . . My arm had gone in up to the elbow into my friend's back.

I stood up. For a moment the ghastly scene revolved in front of my eyes, and I felt as if I was going to faint. I raised one hand to my forehead; it was red. . . . My fingers smeared my face with blood. I had to lean against the wheel of the forge-waggon to prevent myself falling.

A medical orderly had succeeded, meanwhile, in getting two intact stretchers out of the ambulance-waggon, which had also been smashed by the explosion. The doctor, who had been slightly hit himself and was still feeling the effects of the shock, was putting on rough dressings at the side of the road. It took three of us to lift a tall, fair-moustached giant of a driver on to one of the stretchers; he was screaming with pain; one of his feet was nearly severed, and hung loose. We knew there was an aid-post in a farm at the foot of the hill, just outside the wood.

We set off, bending our knees to alleviate the shock of the motion; but one had to climb over detached limbs of horses, and dead bodies too disfigured to be recognisable.

A wounded man seized me by the leg as we went by. His upturned, bloodless face was surrounded with a thin line of blood which had trickled down from one ear round his neck, as though his head had been cut off. His eyes implored. In a voice of the profoundest supplication he murmured:

"You won't leave me here, old man?"

But it was impossible for us to carry two men at once. I looked down at him.

"Some chaps'll be along in a moment with the other stretcher. They'll pick you up. There now, let go of my foot. . . ."

We moved away from the scene of carnage and began to breathe more freely.

The tight canvas of the stretcher retained the blood of the wounded driver, so that his foot lay in a red pool.

He was suffering like a man crucified, twisting his arms about and groaning.

"Oh, my leg! . . . You're jolting me. Ah, how you jolt! Go slower, boys, slower," he gasped.

In spite of all our efforts we could not avoid the shocks that tortured him, and he went on muttering, in gradually sinking tones:

"Slower . . . slower . . . go slower."

His lips went on silently repeating, "Slower . . ." until a rougher jolt made him cry out loud.

In the road in front of the farm where the aid-post was established some medical officers had arranged an operating-table in the shade of a tree. The wounded were put down in a line beside it. A fat doctor with four stripes was running here and there examining them.

Our own wounded began to arrive, walking and on stretchers, alone and supported by comrades. The chin of one of them was a mere bleeding mess. One of his eyes was closed and the other wide open.

The farrier-sergeant's horse, badly torn by a piece of shell, came down the road, following the wounded men. But as soon as it stopped, opposite the farmhouse, it sank down on to its knees. There was human anguish in the beast's eyes. It stretched its head towards me. I put a revolver bullet through its ear. With a thud like that of the stroke of an axe cutting into the heart of a tree, the horse fell over on to its side, and rolled heavily down the bank into the meadow at the bottom.

On the way back, as we left the open air and sunshine and returned into the wood, the thought of what I was going to see again horrified me. And the increasing gloom of the forest, as evening drew on, still further weighed on my spirits.

"Come on!"

Two saddle-horses, with bleeding wounds, were instinctively moving away from the scene of death.

They went down the road with little, short steps, making for the sunlight. The dead horses had been taken out of their harness and dragged to the lower edge of the road. But two men still lay in the middle of it. Someone, by force of habit and out of respect for the dead, had pulled a branch off a tree and covered the two faces with leaves.

The streams of blood in the ruts and gutters had congealed. The warm smell still lingered, shut in by the vault of foliage overhead, and the effect of it seemed even more horrible and heart-rending. In the effort of unharnessing the horses and clearing the road the intestines had been dispersed. They were now lying coiled and covered with dust at as much as several yards' distance from the gaping, entrailless carcases.

Two prisoners, tall men made still taller by their long grey cloaks and spiked helmets, came down the road from the high ground in front. The infantryman who escorted them, fearing that the sight of so much carnage would bring joy to the enemy, had bandaged their eyes. He guided them by hand through and past the corpses. But the Germans recognised the smell of blood. Their brows contracted in a wrinkle of uneasiness, and they sniffed the air nervously.

MONDAY, *September 14th.*

Good weather-proof barns, with plenty of hay in them, sheltered us for the night at Attichy. But our sleep was disturbed by hideous nightmares. I rolled among mutilated corpses, in rivers of blood. In the morning it was raining.

A peasant with drooping, fair moustaches brought us beer and wine in buckets. He lived in an isolated house that could be seen from our billet, on a slope among trees. During the enemy occupation he had left his lonely dwelling and come to live in the village. The day before yesterday, after the departure of the enemy, he went back to his home, accompanied by a French soldier. They were approaching in single file, the peasant in front, when, through the broken-in doorway, he saw a helmeted German, who pointed his rifle at him. He jumped aside, uncovering the French soldier, whereupon the German immediately dropped his rifle and put his hands up. The two of them seized him, sat him down on a chair in the kitchen, and shot him through the head. Then they left him, still in the chair, with his head lolling and the blood running down between his legs on to the tiled floor, while they reconnoitred the surroundings of the house and garden. They found nothing. When they got back the kitchen was empty; there was nothing left but a pool of blood in front of the chair. But there were red drops by the door and on the stairs, and they heard groans coming from the loft above.

"And what did you do with your Boche in the end?" we asked the man.

"He's still in my loft," he answered calmly.

"You'll have to get him out of it. He'll stink."

"Yes, I'm going to dig a hole this evening by the side of my dunghill."

And when I said that instead of killing the German in that brutal fashion they might have made him a prisoner, since he had surrendered:

"Oh," the man answered, "and wasn't he going to kill me if I'd been alone? And me not a soldier, either." And he added:

"You can't do in enough of the swine."

The wind had increased, and it stopped raining. The brigade moved off down the Compiègne road, parallel with the river. But at the end of a mile or two we halted in column. It was decided to do some cooking, but there was no water; I looked everywhere in vain for a spring or a well. There was nothing for it but to fetch the water for soup from the Aisne. A dead German lay among the reeds over on the other side, up to his belly. Well, the water would have to be boiled anyhow. . . . One must eat.

Towards night a mounted orderly came with a message, and we at once moved off at a trot.

Along the side of a high wall a troop of spahis, under their burnouses, made red patches in the twilight. Their little horses stood motionless close beside them in their complicated harness. An Arab, with the fine, regular mask of a statue, was standing with his back against an apple tree. Under the purple woollen hood his brown features expressed that calm melancholy in which the men of his race seem always to languish when far from their desert sands, and the effect of which is both heart-rending and noble. His great, dark, indifferent eyes, staring fixedly into the distance, had an inward regard. He looked cold. The gunners smiled, hailing him as they went by:

"Greetings, old Sidi!"

But he never stirred, and a condescending blink was his only answer.

When the batteries moved into a firing-position the waggons drew up behind a screen of acacias. Except for the low rumble of fighting in the distance the silence of the falling night was absolute, when suddenly, as at a given signal, came the roar of more than forty French guns, almost simultaneously belching a formidable burst of fire across the plateau.

The great flashes lit up the deepening twilight. The air vibrated continuously. It was as though vast, angry waves tossed and crashed together in the atmosphere, like the waves of a stormy sea. The earth trembled in response to the huge vibrations. The darkness gradually increased.

It was evident that the brigade was firing at a fixed and known objective. The enemy retaliated only feebly and at long intervals.

Soon the news was passed from mouth to mouth:

"The Boches are entraining! We're shelling a station. . . ."

"If you ask me," said a reservist, lying on his stomach at the head of his team, carelessly, "I'd let 'em take their tickets in peace. Leave them to it, *I* say. The sooner they clear off the better, and then we can go back home. I've got a wife and two kids, and I don't see the fun of war. . . ."

It was night when, one by one, the guns ceased fire. In a few seconds there was silence, a silence that was disquieting after that appalling cannonade.

We rejoined our batteries. Noiselessly, one behind the other, the guns and limbers vanished like ghosts into the darkness. The soft surface of the field, under the wheels, gave a curious impression of wadding. The diffused, floating clarity of the night was not enough to reveal the nature of the field, over which the long column rolled away without a jolt, without a click from a shoe, with no sound at all but the occasional grinding of badly oiled wheels.

There was an odour of death clearly perceptible in the night air. In the far distance a conflagration showed as a fixed red point. The vast looming trees of a neighbouring park had an inexpressibly disturbing effect.

The wheel of my limber passed over something soft and springy, which gave under the weight. I felt sure it was a body, and turned to look behind, but could make out nothing. A shudder penetrated to the marrow of my bones, in that field of wadding, in the almost clear yet moonless night.

We halted on the outskirts of a village which I guessed to be Tracy-le-Mont. The transport was waiting for us there. Ration-parties were summoned. The men, in their cloaks, formed a dark ring round the waggon, which was lit by a single lantern. I found Hutin and Déprez among them. A voice was calling out the different gun-numbers:

"No. 3! . . . No. 4!"

"No. 1!" called Hutin.

"You've missed your turn. You'll have to wait till the last."

While he waited, we talked. He was very tired and hungry.

"We'll have a good feed," he said; "there's a ration of fresh meat as well as the bread."

"Yes, but we shan't be allowed to light a fire."

Then he abruptly asked:

"Seen anything of the postman?"

"No; why?"

"He turns up more often at the waggon-lines, doesn't he?"

"Then you still believe there is such a man?"

"Ah, you're right. He never comes at all, blast him! Hell, if one only got a letter now and then the time'd go more quickly. The last I had was to say they hadn't heard from me. It's the devil!"

A voice called:

"No. 1 gun!"

"Here! . . . See you later, old man. I'm off after the bread. Try and get back to us soon."

TUESDAY, *September 15th.*

A fine morning. It rained in the night, but we pulled armfuls of straw from some haystacks and put them round the parked guns. I lay down under a limber, which sheltered me half-way down to the knees, and spread a pile of straw over my feet. The ground was fairly dry, and I slept well in spite of the downpour.

At sunrise the sky cleared. The air was warm; the great trees of the park, in all their infinite variety of greens, stood out clearly silhouetted against the pale blue of the sky. The short grass was sweet and fresh.

But here and there, in the fields, one's attention was caught by dark objects. They were German corpses. Once one has seen two or three, it becomes an irresistible habit to look for them everywhere. A forgotten sheaf of corn in the distance looked like one for a moment.

It was still early when we left. The wheels of the vehicles in front made a well-defined road in the soft ground. By the side of it a dead German lay stretched. Some of the limbers had grazed him. Our own came within an ace of crushing his feet. His face was still a bluish yellow. Only the sockets of his eyes, which were closed, had begun to turn green. There was a virile beauty about the grave, rugged mask.

The comrade who sat by me on the limber looked at the face as we passed, and was struck by its expression.

"Poor devil," he observed.

I also was affected by the sight, and said:

"Yes; poor devil. . . ."

But the driver next in front of us, who had a wife and children at home who, for all he knew, had barely enough to eat, turned round in his saddle and jerked out:

"Filthy swine!"

This morning the battle was renewed early with extreme violence, along a front apparently extending from east to west. As far as the eye could see the sky was dotted with shell-bursts.

"And we thought they were entraining! . . . clearing out! . . . Look at 'em now . . . blast their souls!"

"Yes, look. . . . Not much entraining about that!"

Bitterly the men made fun of their yesterday's credulity. But I well knew that they were perfectly ready to believe, if anyone told them so positively enough, that the Russians had reached Berlin.

We learned the truth from some passing infantry: the Germans had entrenched themselves in a formidable manner along some wooded heights and in quarries. The pursuit was at an end, and a new battle had begun.

I asked a sergeant:

"Surely it can't be the ones we were chasing yesterday and the day before who are holding us up now?"

"No," he answered. "No doubt it'll be others, who have been advancing from Belgium in rear of them."

The waggons halted in a narrow ravine, and thence, every hour or so, fed the battery, which was in position near a large farm, and emptied waggon after waggon of ammunition. The German artillery swept the intervening high ground, and salvos of five-nines, intended for a neighbouring cross-roads, but overshooting the mark, threatened to enfilade us at any moment. Elsewhere a battery of seventy-sevens[1] began shelling a wood near the forward exit from our ravine. To cross the high ground became impossible; the enemy had it under observation, and would have found us the easiest of marks. Lieutenant Boutroux, commanding the waggon-lines, was in a quandary. He eventually decided to run the gauntlet of the seventy-sevens. Our waggons accordingly filed along the edge of the wood. Shrapnel burst above our heads. A little farther along

[1] *I.e.* German field guns, having a calibre of 77 mm. Known to the British soldier as " whizz-bangs."

A street in Soissons, September 1914.

the ravine curved sharply, and the danger-zone was passed. Moving along tracks invisible to the enemy, we got away into another position in a similar ravine.

While there we ran short of water. A party of us went off in quest of some along a cart-track that led to a group of barns. There were two cisterns there, into which the rain-water from the roofs collected. A ladder stood against one of them, and out of curiosity I climbed up it to look in. The inner surface of the tank was covered with rust, and from the shallow, muddy liquid emerged an old boot, a felt hat, and numerous doubtful bits of cloth and metal, all slimy with green mould. Such as it was, however, we had to be content with that water. . . .

The noise of the firing gave no indication of any decision having been reached. It neither approached nor receded. Passing wounded told us that the infantry had been held up by immensely strong trenches, despite repeated assaults. The cannonading only died down in the evening when, as soon as darkness hid the high ground from the enemy's observers, we rejoined the batteries. An invisible machine-gun was still firing near by. Fine but penetrating rain began to fall. We had to bivouac in the open, in a beetroot-field. The ground was soft and the wheels sank in it. The horses were not taken out of the traces.

Sleep was almost impossible. One no sooner settled down before one's teeth began chattering and one's limbs trembled all over. One was half afraid of dying of the cold, which ran down one's back in great shivers, if one succeeded in falling asleep.

I curled myself up on my limber like a dog, with my feet hanging over one wheel. The icy contact of the metal was preferable to the wet ground. The rain began to fall more heavily.

WEDNESDAY, *September 16th.*

Very early in the morning a single, dull explosion, far away, first set the echoes rolling. And at once, as though from the lighting of a train of gunpowder, all the guns on the plateau roared into action.

Astruc came up to me.

"Just listen while I tell you what happened to me in the night," said he. "It was like this . . . there wasn't a single place left under the limbers. I saw a great long devil, six feet of him, lying in the open field under a blanket. 'If there's room for one,' thought I, 'there's room for two.' So I lifted one edge of the blanket and crawled in and lay down next to him. But in my sleep I kept pulling more and more of the blanket round me and off him. . . . The next thing I knew, this long bloke was sitting up, wide awake, and shaking me. . . . At first I said nothing . . . lay like dead. That's how I felt, too, tired as a log. But he wasn't having any. 'What the —— are you at?' says he. 'Answer me, you ——!' 'No need to make such a row,' says I. Then I rubbed my eyes and sat up. D'you know who it was? It was the major! . . . I'd pulled the blanket clean off him! . . . I wasn't proud any more, I can tell you. I told him I was so sick I could hardly move, and that the chaps had taken all the room under the limbers. . . . Well, he mumbled something or other, Lord knows what. And I thought a bit, and then just got down to it again by the side of him. And then he said, 'G—d damn it,' says he, 'don't take the whole of the blasted blanket, anyway!'"

The battery took up a new position. The waggons returned to the same ravine in which they were yesterday.

My wrist is giving me a good deal of pain. The cut,

in spite of the bandage round it, has got poisoned by the blood of the killed and wounded at Attichy.

The postman arrived with a packet of letters.

Someone remarked:

"They think at home it'll last till the New Year."

"But the Russians?"

"Ah, the Russians!"

"Let's see then: there's October, November, December . . . three and a half months still to go. . . . We'll be all dead with misery before then!"

Less than five hundred yards away a large group of farm buildings burst into flames under the German shelling. The walls round the garden made a massive rectangle of clean masonry against the bare background of beetroot-fields. The smoke at first curled in thick, dark clouds, lit up by vivid gleams of fire, and then shot up into the clear sky in a tall, straight column.

We knew there were some sheep there. The shelling stopped. I felt that if I could save a joint or two from the conflagration they would make a welcome addition to our monotonous fare. Two men of the 12th Battery, whose waggons were next to mine, had the same idea.

Without delay we started off towards the farm. The field across which we had to go had been ploughed up by German shells yesterday. The enemy had doubtless supposed that our infantry might make use of the cover afforded by the buildings as an assembly-point, and had rained death and destruction all day to no purpose on the beetroots.

One of my companions observed:

"They might have been making holes to plant trees in in quincunxes."

And he added:

"Very neat work it is, too. I'm a gardener, and I know what I'm talking about."

At the edge of a large shell-hole, among the scattered clods, lay the bodies of two gendarmes. One of them, a tall, red-haired man, had a great wound in the chest, and his right arm was curiously bent so that it seemed to have two elbows. The body of the other, a grey-headed corporal, seemed untouched. Only, where one of the eyes should have been there was nothing but a clot of blood; the eye itself, a blue eye, was hanging across the temple at the end of a white tendon.

"Poor old devil!" murmured the gardener-gunner.

He bent over the corpse, with its single eye staring horribly at the sky, and piously covered it with the silver-laced képi that lay near its dead owner.

Tongues of flame were shooting up from behind one of the still intact blue slate roofs of the farm, but disappeared, as we approached, in gathering clouds of smoke. A tall, conical-shaped fir tree, with something funereal in its aspect, towered majestically above the conflagration.

We found two horses and two gunners lying by the side of the boundary wall. They had not been dead long. Their blood was still wet on the ground. I recognised one of the men as one of our senior officers' orderlies. The other lay on his face, with his arms stretched out.

A shell had made a big hole in the courtyard. Three ducks, in spite of the burning heat, were dabbling in a little green pond by a triangular dunghill. A fourth lay by the water's edge with its head blown off.

The framework of a barn stood out like an armature of glowing metal against the vast black curtain of smoke, which from where we stood shut out half the heaven.

Great flames were shooting from the doorway and playing round an abandoned cart and harrow. A pulley high up on the wall, for raising the hay up to the loft, was red-hot. The noise of gun-fire had become almost inaudible, being overcome by the crackling flames and the hiss of sparks falling into the pond. One of the ducks, pricked by a burning fragment, shook its feathers.

"We're none too soon," said the gardener. "The sheep'll be half cooked by this time."

And their shed, when we found it, was only separated by a bakehouse from the burning barn. It was full of smoke, and the backs of the beasts inside were themselves like lumps or flakes of denser smoke. The door was open, and the sheep had made no attempt to escape; they were huddled against the inner wall, under a window that communicated with the bakehouse, from which they were being gradually asphyxiated. They were pushing and straining as if they wanted to break the wall in with their heads.

"Now, then," said the gardener. "You stand there, Lintier . . . by the door. Here's how we'll do it: I and my pal dash in and fetch out one each as quick as we can manage . . . and then you plug 'em in the head at once. See?"

"Right."

The two men disappeared into the smoke and I heard a confused tramping in the shed. A moment later one of them emerged hanging on to the tail of a fat sheep, dragging it along backwards. I shot the animal as it crossed the threshold, and another immediately afterwards. The gardener went back for a third.

I put my revolver back in its holster, and each of us hoisted a sheep on to his shoulders, holding it by the slender legs in front so that the carcases were draped on us like heavy fur cloaks. The dangling heads bled down our backs behind. So laden, we set off across the fields on our return journey.

Suddenly the gardener cried:

"Listen! . . ."

We stood still.

"Down, quick!"

"They've spotted us!"

The noise of the approaching salvo rose to a scream. We flattened ourselves behind the sheep, using them as cover. The shells burst between us and the farm. We at once got up and, in spite of our loads, made off at the double. Passing the dead gendarmes again, we only stopped when we reached the cover of a line of poplars. Three more shells fell on the spot we had just left.

Taking advantage of every tree and fold in the ground that offered cover, we reached the lines without further mishap.

I resumed my place on a bundle of faggots near the fire, while a gunner who was a butcher in civilian life methodically cut up one of the sheep, having hung it up by one leg over a wheel.

Later, while leading the horses to the cisterns to water, I took a short cut across the fields, in the hope of finding potatoes, beetroots, or perhaps onions; onions are what we chiefly need. We have no other means of giving a flavour to our generally insipid rations.

I found neither onions nor potatoes. I found nothing but dead infantrymen, lying among sheaves of corn on the reverse side of a slope. They were visible from afar by their red trousers. They had fallen in the fighting of the 12th.

There were German corpses also in a hollow close by. Thirteen Frenchmen and seventeen of the enemy lay there, almost side by side: yet the French seemed the more numerous. It was a sad sight to see the splashes of red against the yellow corn. The Germans hardly showed.

The arms and equipment of the dead men had been salvaged. Cloaks, coats and shirts had been unbuttoned to get at their identity discs. Their eye-sockets and the tight skin over the muscles of the necks and bare chests were already turning green. A little sergeant, who had fallen on his back with his head pillowed on a sheaf of corn, had one arm raised in the air. There was something acutely painful about the stiff, clasped fingers. The gold stripe on his sleeve glittered in the sun.

As I moved away, low-flying swallows, a sign of coming rain, seemed to graze the corpses with their pointed wings.

THURSDAY, *September 17th.*

Morning found the waggon-lines still in the same ravine, the battery not having moved. Although it had fired more than five hundred rounds in two days, the enemy had been unable to locate it.

The battle raged with increasing violence, and extended towards Tracy-le-Mont, Tracy-le-Val and Carlepont in front of us, Compiègne to the west, and Soissons, or even further up the Aisne, to the east.

All we knew was that we were neither advancing nor retiring. We had begun to fall into a regular routine, having dinner and watering the horses at fixed times.

At the cisterns this morning I saw a remarkable priest. He was on horseback among a group of gunners and supply corps men, whom he was addressing. He was booted and spurred. A long waterproof cape, strapped across his shoulders, hung down over the crupper of his horse; a large wooden cross was suspended from his neck over the polished belt of his revolver-holster, and he had a German bayonet stuck in his broad black belt.

Standing in his stirrups, and stroking his horse's neck, he looked like a warrior-monk out of the Middle Ages.

"Yes, he's a good beast," I heard him say; "a uhlan's horse. I found him after the battle last week near Nanteuil. I was on my way to confess some fellows, and he was running about loose, so I took him. It's a lot better than walking."

And he went on:

"He saved my skin for me yesterday. . . . I had started out for the front line, where they'd been fighting and where I'd heard I was wanted. I was by myself. And I ran into a patrol of uhlans. They had a shot at me . . . and missed. It made me angry not to be able to go where I wanted; so, as I pulled my horse round, I let fly with my revolver. All wrong, I dare say, for one of my cloth. . . . It was more than I could stand, though. I saw one of them tumble off. The others came after me, but this horse of mine went like the wind. . . . They gave it up and left me, so then I turned round and went on again behind them. I found the uhlan I had brought down. He didn't understand a word of French, the great oaf! . . . But anyway, I fixed him up with his absolution before he died. Only just in time, though."

At nightfall we rejoined the battery. It was raining. We wondered whether we were in for another night out in the mud.

I found Hutin, Millon, Déprez and my other comrades of No. 1 gun covered with dust and powder and haggard with exhaustion.

"Well?"

"We've had a bloody day, old man," said Hutin. "I don't know how we're still here, and that's the truth. . . . I'm damned if I do. Ask Millon. . . ."

Millon nodded without a word. He seemed at the end of his strength.

"Gratien's gone."

"Ah!"

"Killed getting on to his horse . . . a piece of shell in the backbone. He never moved. . . . A shell came through the shield of No. 3 gun. It didn't burst. . . . By G—d, if it had! . . . And another fell not six feet from our trench."

"That one burst all right, though. Fairly shook us to pieces. . . . It singed my hair and beard."

"And no one hit?"

"No one in the battery, except for Gratien. . . . Yes, Pelletier had his forehead grazed. Come and have a look at the limber; it's like a sieve. It began smoking. Fun if it had gone up! . . . It was full at the time . . . thirty-six rounds in it. . . ."

Lanterns were lit. A voice came out of the darkness:

"11th Battery, to billets!"

"What's that?"

"Here you are, this way!"

"No. 1 gun. . . . No. 5!"

"This way, No. 5!"

"Billets, 11th! This way!"

We followed a man with a lantern. When we reached our billet we found that we had to share it with some infantry from the Midi, with accents that smelt of garlic.

While the men who had been in action sank down at once into the straw like foundered horses, I myself, having secured a place in the warmth, set off in quest of something to eat and drink with two men of the waggon-lines.

The street was full of obscure crowds of elbowing men and waggons and horses trampling and clattering in all directions over the greasy cobble-stones, to an accompaniment of shouts and noisy breathing. We came to a little café, near which a shell had made a hole in the road earlier in the evening. It was full of marines, zouaves and supply corps men.

A copper lamp with no shade to it, shining through a screen of bottles, jugs and glasses on the counter, threw great shapeless shadows on the walls of the narrow, smoke-filled room, from which came a loud babble of talking, laughing and drinking. There were still liqueurs and rum to be had, and the exhausted soldiers were quickly drunk with alcohol, tobacco and stories of the fighting.

In the vast weariness of the surrounding night, where in barns and lofts and on the bare ground thousands of prostrate men lay as fast asleep as their dead comrades on the battlefield, the little place seemed a haven of refuge, an oasis of light, warmth and oblivion.

A bottle of champagne was found for us. Never had the sparkle and froth of the wine seemed so delicious.

When we returned to the billet everyone was still awake. In spite of loud complaints from the gunners, the infantrymen were still shouting and swearing at one another in their harsh southern accent, and leaving the door open. . . .

"*Will* you go to sleep!" bellowed the voice of a gunner from the inner darkness.

"Hold your blasted noise!"

"Hey, put a stopper on it, Tartarin!"

Men climbed over our feet and stomachs, and dropped their rifles and packs on us. Oaths and recriminations burst forth. It must have been nearly midnight when Moratin, thoroughly enraged, shouted at the top of his voice:

"Just listen to me, you God-forsaken centipedes! Either you stop your filthy goings on this minute, or I'll go and fetch an officer!"

A storm of fearful oaths and insults rose from the straw. The gunners responded in kind. Men who had been on the point of falling asleep shouted:

"Shut it up! Put the lid on it! The lid on it!"

FRIDAY, *September 18th.*

At break of day, as we moved across the plateau along roads deep in chalky mud, we passed large groups of walking wounded: tirailleurs, zouaves, and above all infantry of the line. They walked in the middle of the road, with slow, heavy steps that dragged through the ruts and puddles.

Dawn broke dully. It was about half-past four. The faces of the wounded men could only be made out at the instant our vehicles went by, almost grazing them. There were white bandages, and others that were entirely red. But after each group had passed one saw nothing, in the doubtful twilight, but a slow rise and fall of heads and shoulders.

In the eyes of certain of my comrades, who had seen death at such close quarters yesterday, and who were still tired, stiff and wretched this morning, I surprised glances of envy.

They knew the orders that had come in the night: to return to yesterday's position.

They were not afraid. But familiarity with danger, which had made them brave, did not prevent them from loving life, the life that they felt boiling within them, and which, quite soon perhaps, might be spilt, with all their red blood, over the beetroot-field. They were thinking of yesterday's deaths, of Corporal Gratien, and Captain Legoff, an officer worshipped by his men, and the six gunners of the 11th Battery, reduced to a bleeding, pulpy mass at the bottom of their trench.

For it is at such moments, in the grey, solemn dawns, when the regular jolting of the limbers and the quiet action of the horses, ignorant of where they are going, have lulled one's body half asleep, that the mind fills most sadly and irresistibly with longings for the dreamed-of future, the joys one had looked forward to, all the happiness for which one had hoped the past was a preparation. . . .

The dawn, I know not why, is always an hour of sadness. But to that ordinary sadness there is added, on mornings before battles, the intolerable thought of the terrors and the finalities that the new day may be expected to bring. Longings and fears become obsessions, and commingle and revolve in an endless circle of thought.

To live. . . . To be alive in the evening; but to conquer first. To prevent the enemy from getting past us to our homes beyond, to protect the loved, defenceless beings who are behind us in France, and whose lives are dearer to us than our own. To conquer. . . . To be alive in the evening. . . .

The battery returned to a position near the burnt farm, which was still smoking, while the waggons went back to the same ravine.

My wrist began to be more painful. The doctor wished to evacuate me, but I preferred to rest for a few days where I was, so as to get back to my gun as soon as possible.

The rain began falling in torrents. A horse which we had abandoned yesterday rolled in its death-agony at the end of a field of vetch. The straw which we had gathered, and which had been repeatedly crushed by our wheels and trampled on by men and horses, had formed, with the mud and water that collected in the clayey hollow, a kind of unwholesome manure in which one sank up to one's knees.

The men never opened their mouths except to grouse or swear. There was no more dead wood to be found in the neighbouring copses. It had all been used up yesterday and the day before, and we had nothing to make a fire with. Then some passing gunners told us that there were still a few bundles of faggots left in a farm near the cisterns. We at once hurried off to secure them. The dead bodies were no longer lying in the cornfield on the way there, but in a field beside the road from Tracy, which had become a morass, there was a place where the earth had lately been disturbed, and where two rough wooden crosses had been erected.

The farm to which we were bound had been turned into an aid-post. The outbuildings enclosed a square courtyard, in the middle of which, near a dunghill, the medical carts were drawn up, with their green tilts and red crosses. In one corner a heap of bloodstained compresses, bandages and pads of wadding was slowly burning.

Through the open doors of the sheds and stables one could see sick and wounded lying in the straw under the empty racks and troughs. Some medical orderlies in calico blouses were making soup. A surgeon went by, very upright in his long white operating-robe. There was no sound from any of the wounded.

In the wood-shed ten or a dozen sick infantrymen, with pale faces, were lying on bundles of hay which they had not even troubled to untie. An invisible man, lost in the inner gloom, was breathing hoarsely like an engine.

The cannonade is less fierce than yesterday. But an aviation park has been established a few hundred yards from our ravine, to the rear of some large barns into which the divisional staff moved this morning. Such neighbours are far from welcome. The enemy's gunners are already feeling for the birds perched there in the field. They seem to be firing at random, but their salvos fall, now here, now there, too near us for comfort.

The day drew to a close without any apparent sign of

a result of the battle, which has now been in progress for five days.

But in the evening the long column of the Maroccan Division passed, moving southwards along the road nearest us, towards the Aisne. Large bodies of infantry followed. What this indicated we could not tell, but the sight made us uncomfortable.

Twilight merged into darkness. The great golden beams of searchlights began to sweep the plain. Every hut and haystack stood out fantastically in their brilliant glare, and cast gigantic, inky shadows across the plateau.

Artillery began to go by along the road, also moving south. It was invisible, but we could hear the jolting of the vehicles. And when that ceased at intervals, the wind brought a distant noise as of a torrent, a noise of great waters: it was the tramp of infantry on the march along some other road across the plateau.

It began raining again.

We rejoined the batteries. Waves of men rose out of the night and swept by our limbers. We could see the endless heave of the marching column.

I asked:

"What regiment?"

No answer.

"Hi there, infantry, what regiment?"

A regiment of mutes. . . . They tramped by us into the night without a word.

"What regiment are you? We know French!"

"103rd."

"Where are you going?"

"Don't know."

I asked again:

"Where are you going?"

A voice again replied:

"Don't know."

In the fields by the roadside we became aware of dark,

motionless masses of artillery. Was the Army Corps in retreat? But surely our flank wasn't turned this time? . . . I was in an agony of apprehension.

The rain began to fall more heavily. In the shifting glare of a searchlight the long road showed black with men and horses.

My limber reached its place by No. 1 gun.

"Hutin!"

"Here. Hullo, it's you, old man?"

"Yes. Retreating again, eh?"

"No."

"How not? The whole division's moving south. .

"It's been relieved."

"Can that be true?"

"I've seen some gunners of the corps that's relieving us."

"That means a rest, then?"

"I don't think so. There's talk of a turning movement in the direction of Compiègne and the forest of Laigle, with the Maroccan Division."

Rain . . . night . . . smoking forbidden. The darkness full of distant tramping, hidden rolling of wheels, vague clinking of arms, heavy breathing of men and beasts.

The artillery filed in behind the rearmost line regiment of the division, and a slow march began, interrupted only by the halts of the infantry and such obstacles as were from time to time encountered by the long column.

It was about midnight when we crossed the Aisne. Rain was still falling. Two lanterns were all that indicated the entrance to the bridge constructed by the engineers. It shook under our horses' steps, and we could hear the water lapping against the iron hulls of the pontoons.

On the far side we found the road free. The batteries in front of us broke into a trot. A horse with its leg over the traces held up the waggons for an instant, and, before we could rejoin the column, we were confronted by a cross-roads. In the darkness there was nothing to indicate which road the batteries had taken. We halted, listening. . . . There seemed to be a sound of wheels towards the right, and accordingly we took the road from which it appeared to come. The drivers urged their horses forward. We peered ahead into the night, hoping each moment to see the dark form of a gun or limber loom up out of the blackness. In vain. The road grew narrower. With every yard the risk of going over into the ditch increased. It became all too apparent that we were lost.

The lieutenant gave the word of command to halt, and it was decided to remain where we were till daylight. The downpour redoubled in violence. Shelter there was none. We on the limbers huddled up against one another, and sat motionless, while the drivers dismounted and stamped to and fro in the roadway. My limbs were gradually turning numb with the cold and with the mortal dampness of my clothes, which stuck to my skin like iced cupping-glasses, sucking the warmth out of my blood, when I became aware of footsteps splashing through the puddles past my limber. I made out the forms of some men. Someone, I concluded, had discovered a barn and was guiding them to it. I got down and followed them.

In a very few moments they led me to a house, the dark mass of which suddenly rose before me, blacker than the black night.

My foot knocked against a ladder. Thinking there might be a window at the top of it, I climbed up and found a loft. The floor was rotten and gave under my weight. I clung on to the framework of the low roof.

French infantry defiling before Generals Joffre and Foch, 1914.

There was already a man sleeping there: I could hear his breathing. I cautiously felt about me, and stretched myself out across the rafters, with my head on a beam. The place was almost warm.

SATURDAY, *September 19th.*

At dawn we moved off again. It was drizzling. The road led through an endless forest of tall beeches, from which the collected rain fell in heavy drops, and dead horses lay at frequent intervals in the ditches at the side. Deserted, flooded trenches extended into the undergrowth on either side. Great trees had been cut down and laid across the road, which had yielded under their weight, and when they had been dragged away to make a passage for the troops, their great branches had ploughed up the surface, which the rain had turned into a morass.

In the wan early daylight we went through Pierrefonds, with the rich mass of its castle standing out against the rain-dulled greenery, and entered the forest of Compiègne, where were more water-logged trenches zigzagging in and out among the tall shafts of the beech trees, and here and there deserted primitive bivouacs of ferns and branches; and always dead horses.

The sun, emerging between the clouds and shining down through the foliage, made patches of bright emerald green on the wet mosses, while the bright trunks of birch trees shone out suddenly from among the darker beeches.

Compiègne. There was nothing to show that the town had for several days been in the hands of the enemy. The noise of guns was audible in the distance, to the north-east.

Crossing the Oise, we finally found the brigade again in billets at Venette, an outlying suburb.

In the principal room of a farm into which I went in quest of provisions, the farmer's wife, a matron past her fiftieth year, was describing the horrors of the occupation to four gunners.

She broke off as I entered.

"Have I any milk and eggs to sell? No, no, young man; but I'll give you some. . . . Just a moment."

And she went on with her story:

"Yes, mes pauvres messieurs, as I was saying . . . in front of their father. They tied him up with his back to the wardrobe, so that he had to see it all. There were five or six of them, and an officer. They violated the two girls . . . all the six, one after the other. Two such quiet, refined girls . . . one was eighteen and the other twenty. The poor things screamed and screamed, they say. . . . Ah! they're not men . . . they're beasts!"

And the good woman quietly went on, in natural tones, but lowering her voice a little: "Those weren't the only two. Me as well.

"Yes, me too! You'd think I was too old. . . . I've a son who's a soldier like yourselves. . . . Yes. It was one evening, as it might be now . . . four of them came here to sleep. What was the good of defending myself? . . . It was best to say nothing. . . . There were some who did resist, and they ripped them up. My husband was outside, mending a wheel for them. I thought: If he comes in, what'll happen? He'll try to kill them."

"It's true, too. I should have killed them," interrupted a voice from the obscurity at the back of the room.

I had not noticed the man who was sitting smoking his pipe in the chimney-corner.

The farmer's wife looked round towards him:

"Mon pauvre bonhomme, you might have done for one of them, perhaps, but the others would have killed both of us. And besides . . . well, you see, I'm not of an age that matters. . . . It's what my husband said to me afterwards. . . . One knows there can't be any consequences. . . ."

SUNDAY, *September 20th.*

A long march through a succession of stinging hailstorms, first towards the west, then due north. There is no longer any doubt that we are making an outflanking movement against the enemy's right wing.

MONDAY, *September 21st.*

A serenely luminous early autumn day. We resumed our outflanking march at dawn.

At about midday a battery of our own heavies suddenly opened fire not far from the road along which we were moving. At the same moment our officers galloped off to make a reconnaissance, and we presumed we were going into action ourselves.

Finally, however, we were not needed, and came on to Ribécourt, where we have bivouacked in a park. The guns and limbers are drawn up on a lawn, along the edge of a plantation of beeches bordered with rhododendrons.

There was a brilliant sunset. It reddened the unruffled surface of a piece of water in the park, while in the opposite direction, through a vista of great trees and terraces festooned with virginia creeper, the dark mass of the handsome modern château to which the park belongs gradually faded into the dusk. A little rustic bridge, straddling a stream, showed a curiously Venetian profile against the rich, verdant background.

The night is warm. We have scooped holes for our bivouac fires at the edge of the water, under some chestnut trees. The lake is as black as ink in the darkness, and the bright glow of the fires dazzles one's eyes, so that it is impossible to tell where the water begins. I had to feel my way step by step just now, or I should have fallen in.

TUESDAY, *September 22nd.*

We slept on straw in some outhouses.

My wrist being practically cured, I went back to duty with No. 1 gun.

In the early sunlight the surface of the lake seemed of white-metal. The little Venetian bridge struck a clear note among the sombre foliage, and the water beneath it, flowing over mud and dead leaves, was quite black. The silhouette of the château stood out clearly against the pale sky, and the light gravel of the paths and the brilliant red of the virginia creeper relieved the uniform green of the smooth lawns.

By the time the battery moved off, the rattle of rifle and machine-gun fire was clearly audible through the thunder of artillery. It was evident that the enemy was resisting our outflanking movement and making a stand, and that the time had come to press home our attack. We marched in a northerly direction again, towards Roye. The success of the manœuvre naturally depended upon numbers; the question was, Were we in sufficient force?

On the way we passed a battalion of Senegalese tirailleurs, fine, ebony men in sea-blue uniforms, making coffee by the side of the road, with the simple gestures and admirable attitudes of a primitive race.

We halted under cover of a bank, in a wide valley near the village of Fresnières, which was being heavily bombarded by the enemy. Our officers rode off across the beetroot-fields to reconnoitre.

The line of battle, making an angle in front of Compiègne, ran at this point due north and south. As the crow flies, we were not more than a few kilometres from the positions we had been occupying on the Aisne, near Tracy-le-Mont.

Some peculiarity in the lie of the land caused endless echoing, and made it difficult to locate the exact whereabouts of the main action. Fighting was certainly in progress to our left, in the direction of Ribécourt and Lassigny. The enemy heavies stopped bombarding Fresnières, and yellow puffs of shrapnel began bursting over the sparse trees immediately to our right. Farther away, from behind some woods, rose columns of black smoke, whether from shell-bursts or a fire it was impossible to tell.

But it was towards the north that our most anxious glances were directed, where lines of poplars masked the horizon, and where the presence of the enemy was only revealed by occasional short bursts of rifle and machine-gun fire. Could he be countering our manœuvre to outflank him with a similar movement of his own?

We next observed considerable movements of troops near some wooded ground to the north-west of us. A long column of artillery crawled in a dark line across the fields. A far-away squadron of cavalry, moving at a trot, looked like some strange, wriggling reptile. Then the whole landscape seemed to stir. From where we stood, it might have been merely the undulation of the beetroot-leaves in the wind. Actually, it was a large force of infantry advancing in open order.

Orders came, and we moved into position. The ground under my own gun proved to be extremely soft. There was nothing to stop the recoil, and it was evident that we should be under the necessity of continually relaying, which would seriously retard our fire. No. 2 gun was no better situated; but the rest of the section stood on more solid ground, among stubble. Thus the battery would lose all homogeneity. There was no remedy, however; no alternative positions were available.

The ground to our front was receiving attention from the enemy's field-guns. But we felt little anxiety on their account, for it was evident, judging by their line of fire, that we were hidden from observation in that quarter.

But beyond Lassigny a line of steep, wooded hills rose sharply from the green levels, dominating all the landscape. From these menacing heights our battery was obviously visible, and very nervously we eyed them, wondering what might be concealed in those dark forests.

We were certainly within range of any heavy guns which the enemy might have installed there.

"We want cover," said Bréjard, "and quickly, too."

We hastily dug a trench in rear of the limber. While we were so engaged, a group of seventy-fives in position on our left flank opened fire on Lassigny.

The enemy field-guns lengthened their range and began to look dangerous.

"Stand by!" came the captain's word of command.

"Battery fire, by the right!"

"What range? We didn't hear the range," shouted Millon.

"Eleven hundred!"

"How much?"

"Eleven hundred!"

"Oh! Oh! They're not far off then!"

"Looks bad," muttered Hutin.

With our first shot the recoil carried the gun back more than six feet. It had to be got back into line. But the trail and wheels had been driven so deeply into the ground that our united efforts failed to move it. We struggled and sweated in vain, with our shoulders to the wheels. The men of No. 2 gun had to come to our aid.

Some infantry, meanwhile, moved into position exactly in front of the battery. We waved to them to shift to the left.

"They'll get themselves cut in two, the fools!"

"To the left!"

"What half-baked idiots!"

"Get to the left!"

The lieutenant shouted himself hoarse, waving his long arms.

"Who ever saw such a set of half-wits!"

We yelled in chorus:

"Get to the left . . . the left!"

At last they understood, and moved out of the line of fire.

"Eight hundred!"

We could hardly believe our ears.

"Eight hundred!"

This meant that the enemy was just over the ridge, advancing on us. Yet there were vast numbers of our own infantry over in the direction of Fresnières—why were they not being brought into action?

Moratin, who was standing up on the ammunition-limber, shouted:

"Smack in the middle of them! The last round from No. 1 knocked over a whole heap. Ah! you can see the swine, you can see them!"

This lent new vigour to our struggles with the gun, which was still sinking into the mud with every recoil.

"Hutin!"

"What?"

"Did you hear anything?"

"What sort of thing?"

"There, again!"

"Bullets. . . ."

"Bullets it is!"

"By threes, rapid fire!"

The captain had installed himself in an apple tree under which No. 4 gun stood. The bullets, skimming the ridge in front, were too high to touch us on the ground, but were breaking off the leaves all round the captain. He was begged to come down. One of the men repeated for the tenth time:

"Sir, you can't stay up there!"

The major joined in:

"De Brisoult, come down!"

But the captain, with his field-glasses to his eyes, still looked out towards the north, and very calmly answered:

"I can see beautifully, sir, beautifully. Nine hundred. . . ."

The men at the guns repeated:

"Nine hundred. . . ."

Our infantry had evidently taken Lassigny. Yellow-smoked German shells were now bursting over the town.

"One thousand!"

Our gun had at last found a more or less firm bed, and we were able to fire more rapidly on the retreating enemy.

"Eleven hundred!"

"Twelve hundred. . . . Cease fire!"

This respite gave the men the opportunity to strengthen and protect their trenches with the empty shell-cases that lay in heaps behind each gun. Bullets were still whistling by overhead. But the seventy-sevens shifted away from us. We still crouched at the bottom of our trench. Every five minutes Hutin kept asking:

"What time is it?"

As I told him, he grew more and more restive.

"Damn it," he muttered again and again; "this out-flanking movement isn't working."

In the afternoon orders came from division, and the major ordered up the waggons.

The teams came along at the trot, with the drivers mounted.

"Dismount!" shouted the captain.

They didn't hear. The bullets were still hissing through the air above us, and the drivers' heads would be in the danger-zone in another minute.

"Now then, all together," ordered the sergeant-major. "One . . . two . . . three . . . *Dis-mount!!*"

Twenty voices bawled together. And this time they heard. Without arresting the movement of the teams, the drivers jumped down and ran alongside.

The battery had scarcely moved into its new position, in a field of long grass between two lines of poplars, still closer to the enemy, when the seventy-sevens which had been searching for us all morning without success began bursting very nearly overhead. It was impossible for the enemy to have seen our move. . . . There was no aeroplane up. Could there be a spy watching us and communicating with them?

An infantryman came by, with his hands to his stomach. He was hopping from one foot to the other in acute agony.

"Is there an ambulance along here?"

"Are you hit in the stomach?"

"No, it's a bullet gone through my parts; it burns, ah, how it burns!"

"Listen," said Millon, "go to our waggon-lines. They're over there, to the left, behind those trees. They've got nothing to do. They may be able to help you along a bit."

"Thanks, I'll go straight there."

"But look out between the rows of trees in the meadow. It gets pretty warm there every two or three minutes, when the stuff comes over. . . ."

The wretched man went off, doubled up and twisted with pain.

The captain had taken his stand at the foot of the foremost poplar, whence he was observing. An extended line of men, ready to transmit his orders by word of mouth, occupied the open ground between the battery and the command-post.

The seventy-sevens were now bursting right over us. Each man took cover as best he could. At intervals of about a minute the position was swept by showers of shrapnel bullets, which rattled against the steel armour plating. We crouched motionless; no one had been hit as yet.

Suddenly I saw Hutin—who was in his position on the layer's seat, up against the gun-shield—jump to his feet.

"Good God!" he cried; "the captain!"

Anxious voices asked:

"Is he hit?"

"One burst right in the tree where he was standing."

In a second, in spite of the danger, every man of us stood up.

"Can you see him, Hutin?"

"No. . . ."

Lieutenant Homolle, the major's little orderly officer, who was quietly strolling back across the open from the command-post, shouted at us:

"Get under cover, will you, blockheads!"

"But the captain?"

"He's all right."

And, taking cover with us behind the limber, the lieutenant added:

"I had a couple in the hip myself . . . they don't penetrate. Only bruise you a little. It has to burst within a yard or two to do any harm. The only trouble at present is, that the captain can't see any Germans to shoot at."

The enemy's fire became increasingly violent. The shrapnel bullets came down on the poplars with a noise like hail; detached leaves, blown by the wind, fell and scattered round the guns.

Then one of the connecting files, the shouters as we called them, was hit in the side, and made off as quickly as he could. Next Astruc, wounded in the chest, was helped away by a comrade, with blood streaming from his mouth.

The rest of us stayed where we were, motionless under the fire.

I felt an unaccustomed itching in my beard, which was of several days' growth. I was afraid there might be lice in it. Hutin lent me his glass; and while I was carefully combing my beard, I felt a sudden burning in my right hand, in which I was holding the glass, and which I had raised for a moment beyond the protection afforded by the limber. At the same instant something hit me hard in the chest. With feverish anxiety I felt about over the cloth of my uniform. There was a rent in it over my breast. I felt myself grow pale. I quickly unbuttoned my shirt and vest . . . there was nothing. The skin was unbroken.

My notebook, letters and purse, placed in an inner pocket, had stopped the bullet. Blood, however, was streaming from my other hand. I had instinctively put the glass in my pocket. That it should have escaped being broken between my clenched fingers was a miracle; for my thumb, I now saw, was a shapeless lump of torn flesh.

"You'll have to go," said Lieutenant Hély d'Oissel, who was crouching by my side.

Then Hutin stood up:

"Lintier!"

He shouted my name in tones of such heartfelt concern that I was moved to the very depths of my being.

"It's nothing, old man . . . in the hand, that's all."

"I'll come and dress it for you."

But the shells were bursting without respite, and I refused to let him leave his place and expose himself.

"Get along quickly now," said the lieutenant.

I ran off across the meadow, with hunched-up shoulders under the bursting shells.

The blood was dripping down on to my leggings and thighs, and glued my trousers to my knees. The bullet had carried a little lump of flesh and sinew from my hand to my chest, where it made a red star.

The noise of an approaching salvo came screaming through the air.

There were two dead horses lying at the foot of a poplar, and I flung myself down in the bloodstained grass between them. The shells burst. A large splinter, with a dull smack, buried itself in one of the carcases that protected me. I got up and ran on at full speed out of the line of fire. My wounded hand was messy with earth and horse's blood.

Crossing an embanked road, I suddenly found myself confronted with the threatening muzzles of twenty French guns lined up in the field on the farther side, and had to retrace my steps.

Behind this motionless artillery, in a beetroot-field, lay a battalion of Maroccan tirailleurs. They were invisible until I was right on top of them.

One of their officers, a captain, stood up and beckoned me to him.

"Come here, gunner, and I'll tie up your wound for you. Have you got your field dressing? . . . In the inner pocket of your waistcoat. . . . My dear fellow, it's in ribbons. Are you hit on the chest? No! . . . H'm, you've been lucky. . . ."

He examined my hand.

"A nasty sight! . . . All messed up with earth and gun-grease, too. . . . You'd better run along and get it disinfected as quickly as possible. . . . I'll clean the worst off with a bit of wadding."

I was out of breath with running. The blood was hammering at my temples and buzzing in my ears. The instinct of self-preservation no longer supported me, and as I stood still while he attended to me, I felt I was going to faint; my legs gave way as if they had been broken at the knees, and the form of the captain revolved in front of me.

"Hold up!" he cried.

He put the spout of his water-bottle to my lips, and gave me a generous mouthful of rum. The effect was instantaneous, and I laughed as I thanked him.

"That's more like it, my lad," he said, and finished tying my hand up.

The divisional ambulances, he told me, were at Fresnières, and I set off again. My hand was like lead. And as I walked across the field, holding myself very erect and stiff for fear of feeling faint again, and for the first time clearly realising that I should soon be in safety, far from the shells and fighting, an immense weariness of war, a need of sleep and silence, a sudden failure of will-power, utterly overwhelmed me. I felt that once I reached hospital I should sleep for days and days.

I wanted to sleep, to sleep, above all not to hear the guns, not to hear anything at all. To live without thinking, in absolute silence. To live after having so often nearly died. And then suddenly I remembered what the tirailleur captain had said: that my wound was dirty and infected with earth and horse's blood. The fear of gangrene and, worse still, of tetanus, a terror of every sort of putrefaction, caught me by the throat and half strangled me.

When I reached Fresnières at last a big shell had just fallen at the gateway of the house being used for the ambulance, and killed a medical officer, a nun and four wounded men. The bodies had been laid side by side on the pavement, with the exception of one, a tirailleur, a black giant of a man, the span of whose outstretched arms seemed incredible as he sprawled in the middle of the shattered roadway. The air was full of the swish of passing shells. In the face of the risk that still threatened me though I had ceased to be a combatant, I felt an instinctive, puerile revolt, as if it was a game which ought not to have concerned me any more now that I was no longer playing.

I went into the courtyard, which was full of stretchers on which lay bleeding men. The worst cases were being laid out by medical orderlies on a large kitchen table covered with floral-patterned oilcloth. Two doctors were rapidly dressing them.

One of these, a fat, dark-complexioned man wearing gold pince-nez, beckoned me to him.

"What sort of wound is yours?"

"Shrapnel."

"Let's have a look. . . ."

He unrolled my bandage. When he removed the compress the blood began pouring out in a stream. He glanced at the wound and made a grimace.

"'Mm. . . . This bleeding'll never do."

He called his colleague over, a man with a beard.

"Have a look at this. . . . Better remove the thumb altogether, eh?"

"No question about it," the other answered.

"Well, that's that. We'll cut it off for you at once," the gold-spectacled M.O. informed me.

"Cut my thumb off?" I cried.

"Bless us, yes, unless you want—— Wait a moment," he broke off.

An infantryman had just been brought in on a stretcher, with blood streaming from his shoulder. The doctor knelt down beside him, and felt feverishly in the torn flesh for an artery to pinch.

I thought:

"Cut off my thumb! . . ."

In another second I had made up my mind. Snatching up a compress and bandage from the table, I bound up my wound anyhow with my left hand and teeth, and without the two officers, who were both occupied with the ligature, seeing me, left the ambulance. I knew that I should find the other divisional ambulance at Canny-sur-Matz, two kilometres from Fresnières.

I bought a flask of brandy at a café which was still open in spite of the shelling. Then, as I walked on, I shifted my revolver-holster over to my left hip, where my sound hand could get at it; for night was falling, and German cavalry-patrols often found their way through the French pickets and outpost line under cover of darkness.

The Canny road made a wide detour, and I decided to go straight across country, guided by the church spire which stood out darkly against the pink sky.

My hand was bleeding copiously, but the brandy, which I drank in great gulps, gave me strength, and I felt confident of reaching the next ambulance.

I saw a number of infantrymen lying in a field, near the symmetrical dome of a haystack; the field was on an upward slope, and their red trousers still showed clearly through the dusk against the yellow stubble. A puff of wind brought a disquieting smell to my nostrils. At the top of the slope, the arm of one of the prostrate forms stuck straight up into the clear western sky.

They were dead. . . .

I would have gone on, but I made out, in the shadow of the haystack, a human form kneeling by one of the corpses. The man had not noticed me. . . . He turned the body over and began going through the pockets. I pulled out my revolver and carefully took aim at the looter, and was just going to fire when a sudden fear arrested me. I could see his movements clearly, but the outline of his body, in the deep shadow cast by the haystack, was indistinct. The thought that it might be a gendarme identifying the dead made me lower my revolver. I shouted to him:

"What are you doing there?"

The man jumped to his feet as though at the crack of a whip, and stood clearly silhouetted against the sky. I could see that he was wearing a flat cap with a wide brim.

He shouted back:

"Minding my own business. . . . You mind yours!"

Next moment he was off, running at full speed and jumping from side to side under the menace of my revolver, like a wild animal in flight.

I pulled the trigger. . . . He stopped for a moment. Had I hit him? A spurt of flame flashed out from his shadowy form, and a bullet whizzed by my ear. But just as he was on the point of disappearing behind a bush I fired a second time. It looked as if the man rolled over into the bush.

It was quite dark when I reached Canny. A red lantern indicated the entrance to the ambulance. There were wounded lying in the gateway, and the courtyard was full of them. Medical officers were at work in a glazed verandah that ran along the front of the house. A dim glow coming from within through the coloured glass revealed vague forms of men lying in straw. When the door of the verandah opened from time to time, a rectangle of vivid light shone out over the ground, and one saw a line of stretchers, and the drawn features of the most serious cases waiting to be dressed. Two bearers lifted the nearest stretcher and carried it in. Then the door closed and the courtyard was in semi-darkness again.

I stood watching the scene for some minutes in a state of dazed exhaustion. My hand was still bleeding, but only in drops now.

A stretcher-bearer came by, and I asked him:

"Can you tell me when my wound can be dressed?"

"Later on to-night. Lie down in the straw for the present."

I lay down anywhere. A grave, childish voice came from close beside me.

"You wounded?"

A black man was lying next to me in the straw. Two shining eyes were all that I could see of him.

"Yes, wounded, Sidi, old man. You too?"

"Me wound."

He thought for a moment:

"Black men . . wound . . wounded, wounded . . then him kill . . kill . . kill . . Boches . . oh! *là*, *là* . . *couic!* . . Wilhelm! . . ."

"Ah, you know Wilhelm?"

"Wilhelm . . he bad chief . . he many women . . many! . . ah! . . ."

He seemed to be dreaming.

"Him many wives . . big, bad chief . . far away . . he kill his wives . . many . . cut . . *couic!*"

"Why?"

"Him bad . . ah! . . he have big house . . stick up heads of wives . . ."

He sought for words.

"Stick up heads . . many . . high up . . up on roof . . ah! . . bad. . . ."

Being in too much pain to sleep, I listened to the childish babble of the Senegalese.

"Big chief . . heads of wives on roof . . no good . . ah! no good . . long way away . . ah! . . ."

The man began talking in his own language, a soft, droning, sibilant tongue. Probably he was delirious.

I was very cold; but at last a feeling of drowsiness overcame me, and, covering my legs with straw, I fell asleep.

It was still night when I woke up. . . . It was raining, or rather drizzling. I felt colder, and my wound was more painful.

The verandah was still lit up.

I could just make out the great form of the Senegalese, stretched at my side, but there was no longer any sound of his breathing. I put out a hand; his was quite cold. The straw under me felt wet. I found that my feet were in a pool of blood.

I got up. The worst cases had been attended to. A fire had been lit in the kitchen of the farmhouse; on the hearth a pallid Algerian was dozing. An alarm-clock, between a pair of brass candlesticks on the mantelpiece, indicated two o'clock.

My wound was dressed and my arm put in a sling. There was no need, they said, to cut off the thumb. A medical N.C.O. took my name, and pinned a label to the sling with the words: "Deep shrapnel wound in the right hand: to be evacuated sitting."

WEDNESDAY, *September 23rd.*

The main road, eight kilometres of it on foot. A long, straggling procession of men wounded in the head, arms and shoulders. Into the train at Ressons . . . then the interminable jolting of the cattle-truck, which was half full of loaves of mouldy bread . . . fever, thirst. Then at last hospital . . . bed . . . women's hands, the unrolling of the bandage, stiff with dark blood, silence. . . . Ah, the silence! . . .

* * *

On September 30th a letter came to me in hospital from my friend Hutin. I reproduce it in all its simplicity.

September 25th, 1914.

"DEAR OLD MAN,

"Hurry up and let us hear from you. I hope you will soon be out and about. We all send you our best wishes for a speedy and complete recovery.

"Perhaps you haven't heard about the sad thing that happened to the battery, only a few minutes after you left. The captain was killed. A shrapnel bullet under the left eye. You remember how we all used to say, 'If anything happens to the captain, he can count on us.' The moment he fell, all the ten of us ran out to him at once, to help him. It wasn't any good. It was all over with him. We brought his body back to the battery. Lieutenant Hély d'Oissel took command, and we went on firing. He cried as he gave the elevation. At about eight o'clock, when we had orders to leave the position, and sat Captain de Brisoult on the limber of No. 1 gun, half the men had tears in their eyes. Two men held him up between them, with a white handkerchief over his face. At Fresnières we kept watch over him all through the night. He is buried there.

"Since then we haven't done much. Our sad loss has left us in very low spirits. I am not allowed to say where we are. But if I tell you that the battery has hardly moved since you left, you will know about where we are stationed.

"Yours,

"GEORGES HUTIN."

I, too, wept as I read that letter.

FINIS

www.ingramcontent.com/pod-product-compliance
Lightning Source LLC
LaVergne TN
LVHW010941100826
845153LV00002B/112

9781783318346